The Poetry *of*
Dante

GIOTTO'S DANTE

Seymour Kirkup's Drawing, reproduced
by permission from **Frank J. Mather, Jr.'s**
"Portraits of Dante"

The Poetry of Dante

By
BENEDETTO CROCE

Translated by
DOUGLAS AINSLIE

PAUL P. APPEL, *Publisher*

MAMARONECK, N.Y.

1971

CONTENTS

AUTHOR'S NOTE

This work was completed in 1920 and parts of it have already been published in periodicals. Its purpose is to afford a methodological introduction to the reading of "The Divine Comedy." At the same time it is intended as an example of such reading conducted in a straightforward fashion, free from distracting considerations unessential to the theme. If it succeed in removing to some extent the confusion surrounding the general run of Dantean literature and help to focus the attention once more on what is proper and essential in Dante's work, it will have attained its end.

B. C.

CHAPTER I

INTRODUCTION

Is there any reason why Dante's poetry should be read and judged differently from other poetry? Considering the severe traditional profile of Dante, poet, philosopher, theologian, judge, preacher of reforms and prophet, and listening to the epigrams in which he is said to be " equally great as man and as poet," " more than poet," and his " Divine Comedy" unique in literature, we would be tempted to say yes. Not only was he poet and thinker, representative of the ideas of the Middle Ages, but he was also a man of action and shared in his own way in the Italian and European crisis at the end of the thirteenth and the beginning of the fourteenth centuries. His greatest book is very complex, *opus poeticum* being intertwined with *opus philosophicum* and *opus practicum*. In it we find sentiment and imagery, acts of faith and religious acts, instruction, censure of the politics of Florence as well

as those of Church and Empire, and of all
Italian and foreign sovereigns, condemnations
and vendettas, announcements and prophecies;
and in each case allegorical and otherwise con-
cealed meanings are superadded to the obvious
and literal.   Indeed, the tendency to put his
poetry in a class by itself is very natural.

But we shall do well to be on our guard here
against exaggeration; if Dante were not, as he
is, a very great poet, there would be little importance to the details of his life and work.
There were many theologians, philosophers,
publicists, utopians, and political partisans in
his, as in all times.   Furthermore, if much of
the subject matter is important it cannot be
unique.   Scientific and philosophical thought
and practical tendencies and ends are discoverable in every poet and in every poetical pro-
duction. We can also find in many works hidden
allusions and intentions.   In fact, since a poet
is a human being, it is always possible to give
to any poetical work a distinct philosophical and
practical interpretation, such as is made so much
of in the case of Dante.   This interpretation is
different from, and additional to, the true poetic
interpretation.   We can call it, from our present point of view, " allotrious."   It does not

stand to the other in the relation of "historical" to "æsthetic"; both interpretations are
historical, only one is concerned with the history of poetry and the other with another and
different kind of history. To it, Dante's work,
in its admittedly significant philosophic and
practical aspects, affords rich material, far
richer than the work of most poets, some of
whom present almost no material at all for
such interpretation. But the difference between
him and the others in this respect is always
simply one of quantity, and there is nothing
"unique" about him along these lines at all.

Philosophical, ethical and religious interpretation of Dante's work began in his own time
with the notaries, friars, and professors of the
university, and with the sons themselves of the
poet, and would probably have begun with the
poet himself had his life been long enough. The
commentator of his own poetry in the "Convivio" would hardly have left the "sacred
poem" without commentary. Perhaps he
would have developed it along the lines of the
much disputed epistle to Scaliger. At any rate
it would not be easy to imagine a work of
greater usefulness than such a commentary
would have been. It would have spared pos-

terity serious, and in great part useless, labours
in the shape of the many great commentaries
of the fourteenth, fifteenth, and sixteenth centuries, and saved us from the appalling bulk
of Italian and foreign exegesis which scholars
have been engaged upon from the seventeenth
century to the present day. There was a lull
of about two centuries, from the early sixteenth
to the late seventeenth, but the last ten years
have seen the greatest activity of this kind yet
known.

The future historian of Dantean exegesis
will succeed better than his predecessors if he
measure the progress of criticism by the
growth and elaboration of historical method.
Interpretation has become and tends to become
more scientific and critical. At first it was
chiefly moral and religious, as it sometimes
threatens to become again in ascetic and meditative minds. It has, at various times, assumed
that political and national importance, especially
in the period of the Italian Risorgimento, which
it now enjoys almost solely among professorial
and political speechifiers. At all times it has
served as an academic exercise for ingenious
imagination and subtle sophistry, and serves as
such still for idle spirits. But the really fruitful

direction was taken when Vincenzo Borghini
recognised in the sixteenth century that it was essential to the methodical study of Dante to seek
out the authentic documents relating to the
thought and knowledge of his time and to study
the language and customs of his period. Following the students of the eighteenth century,
Carlo Troya, one of the most fruitful of Dante
scholars, in the early nineteenth century linked
Dante with the history of the Middle Ages
and cleared the supporter of Henry VIII from
much untimely ideology.

Studies of the philosophy of Dante, and of
all the speculative currents which he mingled
with his usually Thomistic views, belong to the
" allotrious " researches above described, as
also do those relating to his political ideal. The
same may be said of the resemblances to, and
the differences from, the other ideals proposed
or longed for in his time; his public and private
affairs; his varying thoughts and hopes; the
chronology of his works, and of the different
parts of the " Comedy," in connection with
their historical inspiration; his literary, classical and mediæval inheritance; what he knew of
past and contemporary history; what he believed to be real in the facts to which he al-

luded, and what he held to be simply probable
or imagined altogether for his own purposes;
his views on allegory in general and that form
of it which was particular or incidental to the
poem; whether he considered the end of the
poem to be ethico-religious, or political, or both,
and so on.   Research along these lines has now
gone very far in the hands of the best scholars
engaged in it.   But, in my opinion, it should go a
good deal farther and thus get free of a methodological defect which injures and renders it
more or less frivolous throughout, especially
where it is concerned with allegory.

It is well known that the work which has been
done and is being done in the sphere of allegory
is as little conclusive or fruitful as it is extensive
and cumbrous.   Allegory, for him who does not
lose sight of its true and simple nature, is nothing but a sort of cryptography, and therefore a
practical product, an act of the will, which decrees that this is to mean one thing and that
something else; by " sky " (writes Dante in the
" Convivio ") " I wish to mean science and
by skies, sciences; and by eyes, demonstrations."   When an author does not leave
an explicit document to declare what act of
will he has accomplished, supplying the

reader with the " key " to his allegory, it is
useless to seek or hope to fix definitely the meaning of his work. The " true meaning " cannot
be seen unless the author tells it, as is also remarked in the " Convivio." Wanting the key,
which is the express declaration of the composer
of the allegory, we may, by basing our conclusions upon other passages in the author's works,
and in the books we know him to have read,
arrive in the most favourable case at a probable
interpretation. But we can never be certain.
For certainty we need, strictly speaking, the
ipse dixit. If in the matter of poetry the author
is often the worst of critics, in the matter of
allegory he is always the best. But the majority of the students of Dante's allegories forget
this principle, which is proper to the matter of
which they treat, and claim to reach the hidden
meaning by acuteness of intelligence and indus-
trious reasoning, which they would do better to
reserve for other arguments. Thus they enter,
often without being aware of it, upon a mis-
leading highway of conjectures (though, and indeed because, it is so very wide). Here one
destroys the other and convinces no one, except
perhaps its author, who has allowed himself to
be fascinated by his own conjectures, and then

has reinforced them with his self-love (with "the affection which binds the intellect "), and has put faith in them all the more passionately, the more an obscure consciousness has warned him that he cannot found them on solid ground.

The overvaluation referred to above, or the misunderstanding of the particular importance of Dante as philosopher and politician, is to be referred to this error of method, which gives a truly dilettante character to a great part of such researches. But indeed, even where it at first seems possible to speak with the greatest truth of the originality of Dante's thought, that originality, under proper criticism, becomes gradually attenuated, or ceases to exist. Such is the case with the treatise " De Monarchia." The much praised conception of a world monarchy with universal peace proves to have been a pious hope entertained in all ages. The other original idea believed to be discoverable in it, the idea of a lay state, proves to be only a dualism of the spiritual and temporal powers, implying due reverence for the former by the latter, and ultimately a certain subordination. In fact, the " De Monarchia " is rather the work of a publicist than of a political scientist, although it reveals in its very contradictions the difficulties and the expedients in which the mind of the Middle Ages was engaged, and which paved the way for the future political science of Machiavelli. Approximately the same is to be said of the " De Vulgari Eloquentia " which did not inaugurate modern philology, though it is a work of great importance for the account of the various dialects of Italy which it contains. Modern philology is due, on the contrary, to modern historical sentiment. The " De Eloquentia " contains nothing of a revolutionary character or even of importance for the philosophy of language. It is to be looked upon as a document of value for the study of the artistic formation of Dante, who used it to lay down an ideal of language and of style in conformity with his own way of feeling, the " illustrious common speech " (just as the Florentine speech was the ideal for Manzoni in recent times and in a different sense). The like is true of his metaphysics and ethics in general, where it is only possible, by the exercise of much good will, to find here and there some detail not derived from the books which he had studied.

Researches into the thought and doctrine of Dante consequently, and of necessity, centre around minute details, to which are attributed a

greater value than really belongs to them. The
eagerness with which studies of the Dantean
allegories are pursued is the most evident proof
of this tendency to exaggerate. Even if it were
possible to determine the allegories with certainty, as it is not, and if the elements of an
authentic interpretation did at last make themselves evident, what else could be revealed but
repetitions or, if you like, slight varieties of
concepts, beliefs, designs, expectations, already
known from those places in his works where
Dante speaks without allegory, and from other
contemporary or anterior texts? It is not to
be believed that we should obtain astonishing
revelations, of the kind announced by Rossetti
and some of his followers. But even if we did,
such revelations would be interesting merely as
historical curiosities. They would, too, reveal
a Dante by no means healthy in a certain region
of his mind. We owe it in part to these infla-
tions, to these subtleties, to this disputing about
trifles, and still more to the empty conjectures of
the allegory-hunters, that " Dantist " has come
to mean in ordinary Italian speech " Danto-
maniac." Such things are certainly inevitable,
and are always found in the cult which gathers

round a great man; but we should be glad to dispense with them.

It remains true nevertheless, after making this necessary protest against the too much that is too much, and against partial defects of method, that the " allotrious " interpretation of Dante is not only legitimate, as for any poet, but possesses in his case a particular appropriateness. Equally legitimate is the æsthetic or æsthetico-historical interpretation. Its rights have not, as a matter of fact, been disputed, and could not be disputed save by those who intentionally or involuntarily do not admit art as a reality and treat it as though it were an appearance, resolving it into other spiritual forms or into altogether materialistic conceptions. It too has its long history, which this time does begin with Dante, that is to say with the theory by means of which he explained and judged poetry, and with the definition which he gives of himself as the poet of " rectitude," or the " sacred " poet. In its course it flows into the history of æsthetic and of æsthetic criticism from the Middle Ages up to the present time; and here too progress was effected by means of the perfecting of the concept of art, and the ever greater ex-

actness and firmness of historical intuition.
Praise of Dante as the theologian-poet, knowing dogmas and learned in ethics, was succeeded
by the discussions of the sixteenth century about
the " Comedy," as to whether or not it would
fit into the classification of the Aristotelian
Poetic and how it did so, or whether it were
not an altogether new class in itself,—and so on,
throughout the eighteenth century, to the refutation, negation, and satirising directed against
it in the name of rationalistic good taste.
Thence followed the reaction and correction
that gave warning of the necessity, before
judging the " Comedy," of first placing it in the
medium of the ideas and customs and passions
of the times when it appeared; and this again
was followed, in the romantic period, with a
more lofty and free consideration of the poem,
in conformity with a loftier and more liberal
conception of art.

If the " allotrious " and æsthetico-historical
modes of interpretation are both legitimate,
their conjunction is on the other hand illegiti-
mate, although a scholastic formula often repeated and here directly refuted, asserts that the
condition and foundation of the æsthetic interpretation of the " Comedy " is its philosophic,

moral, political and otherwise allegorical interpretation. This formula once assumed an appearance of truth owing to the false identifica-
tion which, as we have observed, used to be
made of the " allotrious " with the historical interpretation in general; and the æsthetic interpretation used to be made to follow this, conceived as non-historical in itself and finding its
premise or historical basis in the other. But
since both are in their own way historical, that is
to say, correspond to different and complete histories or forms of history, it is clear that their
conjunction as desired is without the necessary
justification. The history of Dante's poetry and
that of his philosophy or his politics have their
roots equally in all the history preceding that
æsthetic creation, that acceptance or reform of
doctrine, that practical action; but each one of
them completes its own synthesis of historical
material, in conformity with its own internal
principle, *ad modum percipientis* or *appercip-*
ientis.

Let truth prevail. In the history of philosophy the doctrines of Dante must be re-
thought in their logic and dialectic and linked
with anterior and posterior doctrines, in such a
way as to cause their truth and error to become

apparent and to make clear the place they held and the function they exercised in the general development of thought. But in the history of poetry, as in the simple reading and enjoyment of poetry, this does not matter; were it introduced, it would cause disturbance, because those doctrines are there, not in so far as thought, but only in so far as they are imagined, and cannot therefore be dialecticised as true and false. They should be known, but in the same way as we know a myth or fable, or any other fact, that is to say, as elements or parts of poetry, from which and not from logic, they derive their significance.

In like manner, in a history of culture in the Middle Ages and in the age of Dante especially, it is important to learn what was known and believed as to certain personages and certain myths, and to discern in the judgments regarding them what comes from criticism, more or less well directed, and what from traditions or fancies or, indeed, misunderstandings: the Roman Empire, Cæsar, Brutus, Cato, Virgil, Minos, Pluto. But in poetry, and therefore in the history of Dante's poetry, these facts and personages become images or metaphors of the different modes of feeling of the poet. It is certainly necessary to know how he thought them, but only in relation to the use he made of them, their colouring of reverence, admiration, love or terror. Dante, either ill-informed or forgetful, may have confused the characters of Cato of Utica and Cato the Censor; but the figure of the guardian of Purgatory is not the fruit of a confusion, it is a poetical creation. The name and certain traits are taken from a remembered Roman hero, who thus contributes a sort of aureole to the character. In this same way we give a name full of dear memories or propitious augury to a beloved daughter. The history of the name certainly does not affect the reality of the person to whom it has been given.

In a political history of Florence, it is indispensable to start from economic and juridicial conceptions and to follow the industries, the commerce, the class struggles, the treaties and the wars, the actions of the King of France, of the Emperor and of the Church, and to understand what problems of a social and international character were then debated, what were the institutions that were losing ground and what were the new ones arising and growing stronger, and on which side lay the greater political sagacity and wisdom. It is also pos-

sible to touch upon the personal actions of
Dante, to the extent allowed by extant documents. We say he was inscribed as prior of the
Art Guild, was an orator, was condemned to
exile, that he was both actor and sufferer in that
process of demolition and construction, of of-
fence and defence. But all this has no direct
connection with the poetry of Dante. The
passionate expressions which seem to be due to
the historical events, and therefore to be intel-
ligible and capable of being judged only in relation to them, are in the poem in the same way
as what is derived from philosophical and historical culture. They are essential parts which
we may not abstract from the images to which
they belong, and examine as social and political
history, unless we wish to destroy rather than
throw light upon the whole. The " new folk "
and the " unexpected gains " are not in the verse
of Dante, as in political history, cause and effect
of the industrial and commercial rise of Florence, but an expression of disgust and abhor-
rence in the mind of the poet. Political history
will judge " the boor of Aguglione and he of
Signa," as Troya suggested, to have been more
sensible or instinctively better directed than
the factious white Guelf, Alighieri, and the

" shameless Florentine women " to have been more patriotic than he; but in the poetry, whatever those characters may have been in reality, they are the object of contempt and indignation, and the boor of Aguglione and he of Signa certainly have " a sharp eye for cheating " and the Florentine women continue to show " both breast and nipples ",—let the priest shame them by pointing to them from the pulpit! In writing history or anecdote, we should examine the truth of the tragic death of the lovers of Rimini, or of the greatness and ruin of Count Ugolino, as recounted by the poet; and it may be that in judging them, as one of the interpreters suggests, Dante allowed himself to be to some extent dominated by his hatred of the Pisans and of the Malatestas, " those black Guelfs." But when reading the episodes, beware of separating what cannot be separated and substituting the results of such researches for the living qualities of Dante's characters! If you do, whatever the characters have of piteous or of tragic disappears at once. Horror at the ferocity of the Pisans vanishes before the recorded crimes of Ugolino, and the love of a Francesca over thirty for a cousin over forty, appears, as indeed it has appeared to one critic, to be nothing but an ignoble intrigue. It appears connected with an intrigue which Dante is supposed to have begun, or to have wished to begin, with his own sister-in-law: and this of that Francesca about whom the god-like power of poetry has woven a new history, a history which made Byron in Ravenna feel such keen delight to breathe the air and made Carducci long for the cypressed hill where she " softened her ardent eyes to smile! "

Finally, to dwell for a moment upon a point that is wont to cause the greatest difficulties, allegory certainly existed among the forms of expression or rather of communication and writing, usual or preferred, during the Middle Ages. It was a hidden mode of communication and writing, a propounding and guessing of riddles, and in order to understand certain thoughts, it is sometimes necessary to decipher allegorical cryptograms, if the means at our disposal permit of their being deciphered. But whatever the investigators and conjecturers as to Dante's allegory may boast or claim, explanations of the allegories are always entirely useless, and in so far as useless, harmful, when considered in connection with the enjoyment of history or

poetry. In poetry, allegory never occurs; it is
certainly talked about, but when one goes in
search of it and hopes to find it, one does not
find it, since it is a vain shadow even in appearance, much more as reality. Allegory is found
in connection with poetry in two cases. First,
when allegory is joined to poetry *ab extra,* when
it has been decreed by an act of will, as we said,
that certain personages, certain actions, certain
words, contained in the poem, should also bear
the meaning of a certain fact that has occurred
or will occur, or of a religious truth, or moral
judgment, or whatever else it may be. In this
case, it is clear that the poetry remains intact,
and that it alone can concern its own history.
The whole of the other, or secondary sense in
which it may be understood—on the basis of
which the poetry would mean nothing in itself
but would be simply an object serving as a sign
—belongs to the sphere and history of the practical activity. The second case is when the allegory does not let the poetry exist or does not
allow it to appear, replacing it with a crowd of
discordant images, poetically frigid and mute,
which for that reason are not true images, but
simple signs; and in this case, since there is
not poetry, there is no object whatever

for the history of poetry, but only a con-
fession of its limits, of poetic failure, of
nothingness and ugliness. A third possible
case would be one where allegory exists, but
allegory so completely translated into images
that it does not remain outside the poetry, as in
the first case, and does not destroy or impede it,
as in the second, but co-operates with it from
within. But such a case would be a contradiction in terms, because if there be allegory, it is
always by definition outside of and distinct from
poetry, and what is really within the poetry,
fused and identified with it, can be no allegory,
but only poetic imagery, which is not limited in
signification to material finite things, but always
has an unbounded spiritual value. In all these
cases, he who reads poetically should never find
the allegorical sense within reach; he navigates
in other, sweeter waters. Further, it is impossible to see side by side two things of which
one appears only when the other disappears.
And it is a sophism to suppose it necessary first
to obtain the allegorical explanation, in order
to understand certain poetical passages. What
should necessarily precede is only the knowledge
of the elements of language, of living language,
which attain to a new synthesis in those pas-

sages. And it is a further sophism to suppose
that the allegorical meaning adds a vague and
pleasing or elevating "suggestion" to the
poetry. A suggestion of what? Of ceasing to
pay attention to the poetry?

An instance of the first (in which allegory is
joined to poetry *ab extra*), is the case of
Beatrice in the last cantos of the "Purgatory"
and of the "Paradiso." She may be, allegorically, all that Dante desired or that interpreters
have imagined (Theology, Revelation, Active
Intelligence, and so on) but whatever she be in
this arbitrary imposition of names, in poetry she
is simply a woman, a woman once loved and now
happy and glorious, yet benign and helpful to
her lover of the past. Or take the case of
Matelda. She has at least twenty doctrinal
interpretations, all the way from Active Life to
Foreseeing, Co-operating Grace, from Perfect
Human Nature to Conciliation of the Church
with the Empire. At least six historical interpretations have been given her: Countess Matilda of Canossa; Saint Matilda of Hacken-
born; Matilda of Magdeburg, a devotee;
blessed Matilda, mother of the Emperor Otho
I; Saint Mary Magdalene; and a friend of the
Beatrice of the "Vita Nuova." But in poetry

she is neither more nor less than she who is pic-
tured for us, and whose voice we hear through
the poet's feeling; a young woman, wandering
in a little wood in the freshness of the morning,
singing and selecting " a flower from amid
the flowers." This figure is infinitely richer in
poetry than that supposed to be made more complete by virtue of secondary meanings and historical allusions. Or take the case of the " four
stars," the four famous stars which Dante sees
all at once in the sky when he leaves the Inferno, and in whose flames the heavens seem to
delight. They may perhaps be the four cardinal Virtues of the allegorists, but in poetry are
nothing but the emotion of wonder and ecstasy
caused by the unexpected and most beautiful
sight.

It is as easy to find instances in the first case,
for they are very numerous, as it is difficult in
the second (in which allegory exists without
poetry). Dante is so robust and fruitful a poet
that he very rarely, and never altogether, confines himself to sterile allegory. Nevertheless,
with this reservation, we may still cite the
Hound which will not eat of earth or wealth,
but only of wisdom and love and virtue, and
will be born between Feltro and Feltro;

the she-wolf which "makes many to live
wretched "; the firm foot " which was ever the
lowest "; the fair rivulet " which can be
crossed " " as though it were solid earth "; and
the like. Certain rather empty sonnets and
odes which vibrate uncertainly between the
moral on the one hand and the amorous on the
other can also be mentioned here. In the
" Divine Comedy," in certain places which pass
for allegorical, Dante is simply remodelling the
prophetic and apocalyptic style, and though this
means that he objectifies his allegory and makes
material of it, it does not keep him from moving
in the sphere of pure poetry at the same time.

It is not possible to give examples of the third
case in which allegory is completely transmuted
into imagery, because it is inconceivable, as we
have already pointed out. When instances of
it are brought forward, we can easily see that
here we have poetry without allegory, or poetry
which, although it endures the presence of allegory, yet has a poetical meaning proper to
itself. A case in point is the ode of the " Three
Ladies." Coleridge said he had read this ode,
he did not remember how many times, but had
never been able to understand it. Nevertheless, he said, it exercised a great fascination

upon him, owing to " that soul of universal
poetry that is in it, in addition to the specific
meaning, as in all real poetry." It is clear from
this, that Coleridge, with his fine understanding
but not equally expert theoretical capacity,
called that which is not specific but extraneous
" specific meaning," and called " soul," or " inspiration," or " fascination," what is the really
specific, because the poetical sense.

In fine, if all the allegories of all the lyrics
and all the passages of the " Divine Comedy "
were accurately explained, it would still remain
for us to interpret the lyrical passages historically. We should have to exclude the allegories
as useless and harmful distractions, and seek out
the true " specific meaning." And if I had to describe somehow the historical interpretation
proper to historico-æsthetic interpretation, or
the analytical moment that precedes the synthetic moment, I should say that it is the *explanatio verborum,* the interpretation of the
meaning of the words in a wide sense. This
meaning, as we all know, is not derived from
their etymology and from the sequence of the
concepts and of the sentiments that have come
together to form it; all this constitutes a pre-
history which has been superseded. It is de-

rived from the custom of those speaking at a given time, and from the context in which the words have been used, and is then determined and individuated in relation to the new phrase in which they appear. The new phrase is composed of them, and is the determining factor in their meaning, at the same time. Philosophical propositions, names of persons, references to historical events, moral and political judgments and so on, are in poetry nothing but words, substantially identical with all other words and are to be interpreted within the limits indicated. In the " allotrious " interpretation they are no longer and must no longer be words, that is to say images, but *things*.

It may happen that it is not always possible to give the precise sense of certain words in the *explanatio verborum*. We may fail in giving the moral, philosophical and general historical content that vibrates in them. The same thing may happen for every word, even for those that are generally said to be common or familiar. But when there is failure to determine such content with exactitude, an obscurity more or less great persists; and there has been much loud talk about the " obscurity " of Dante. It has even become proverbial, so strangely have its importance and extent been exaggerated. The obscurity of Dante is rather a difficulty which arises from the language he employs being very rich and in some parts antiquated, from the historical references being manifold and not obvious, and from the philosophical terminology belonging to a period of philosophical culture that has been outgrown and is known only to specialists. With a little correct information, the obscurity becomes clear enough. In addition, such explanation is only required, as a rule, in relation to special points of secondary importance. Sometimes the obscurity persists, either because the poet has paid but little attention to the avoidance of misunderstandings, or because the documents which should throw light upon his meaning are wanting. In such cases the interpretation becomes merely conjectural, that is to say, several possibilities are admitted, and it would be impossible to be positive about any of them without caprice. But instead of recognising this fact and accepting the inevitable, Dantists attach themselves to the obscure verses with a tenacity which amounts almost to frenzy, never ceasing to propound and dispute new and often eccentric interpretations. They would do better to limit themselves, while

waiting hopefully for the appearance of some
new document, to one of the two following
courses. Either they should treat the obscure
passages like the lost parts of a picture which
cannot be restored, and over which a neutral
tint is spread, or they should adopt what seem
to be the most suitable and most beautiful
among the various interpretations available.
Thus for the verse, "For hunger can do more
than pain " (of Count Ugolino), the interpretation that the pain which held the unfortunate
man alive in delirium was finally overcome by
exhaustion and death, is certainly to be preferred, because this last touch completes a scene
compact of human suffering far more perfectly
than the other interpretation of an Ugolino
who bites desperately into the flesh of his dead
sons. But it is not absolutely certain that Dante
may not, on the contrary, have intended to say
precisely the second of these things, in conformity with the rumour current in some Italian
cities about Count Ugolino's last moments on
earth. Thus too, "The way also displeases
me " is better interpreted as referring to the
death dealt out to Francesca in her moment of
bliss, which made her shame public so that it
still burns into her soul; but it does not ex-

clude the possibility that Dante intended to refer to her lack of time for repentance, or even as others pretend, to the anecdote (the late anecdote) of how she was taken from Paolo and given to Gianciotto by stratagem. And to give a third example, " The heart that still drips upon the Thames " is more efficacious poetically if *cola* be taken (as has been proposed) from *colare* and not from *colere* (honour), and means that the heart still drips blood and has not been appeased with vengeance. On the other hand, it is of no use to insist at all costs upon knowing the precise meaning of the verse, " Whom perhaps your Guido disdained," which alludes to biographical details, altogether or almost altogether lost, concerning Guido Cavalcanti and his relations with Dante. This would be to lose the poetry of the episode by insistence upon an obscure verse. That such is the case, is perfectly clear, and this is one of those instances in which it would be well to resort to the " neutral tint."

The distinction, the profound difference, that we have tried to fix in exact logical terms between the two interpretations, " allotrious " and æsthetic, is generally felt, though expressed in a confused manner and in unsuitable terms. Dislike of the allegorists, the historicists, the anecdotists, the conjecturalists, and of the philologists and " commentators " in general, is sprung from such a feeling or semi-feeling. The proposal so often made, and the exhortation so often preached to read Dante after the commentaries have been thrown away, " as man to man," is also due to this feeling. Certainly the commentaries cannot be dispensed with and no one has ever been able to get along without their aid in reading Dante; but the advice to throw them away is good whenever (and the case frequently presents itself) instead of supplying only the data useful towards the historico-æsthetic interpretation, they exhibit things that are inopportune and have no connection with the subject. No one can read Dante without adequate preparation and culture, without the necessary mediation of philology. But the mediation should lead to our finding ourselves with Dante as man to man, or to placing us in immediate relation with the poetry. There is this much of reason behind all vexed and otherwise unreasonable proposals to abolish the commentaries.

It will be objected that in making the proposed distinction we have cut our Dante into

two or more Dantes, and that this is a more
cruel operation than that which the devil of
the ninth circle performed upon the dissemi-
nators of scandal and schism, and is justly to be
deprecated and prevented. Here, however, it
is not a question of " cutting " anything, but
only of thinking. It is not possible to think,
save by distinguishing; and the distinction which
is here being discussed, was carried out by
Dante himself, when instead of confining himself to politics or philosophy, he allowed himself to be also a poet, interpreting experience
by turns not only in speculation and practical
activity, but far more largely and energetically
in the joy of his verse, in the composition of
sonnets and odes, and in the miraculous " Comedy." No unity could exist in him outside of
this dialectical movement. A Dante in himself
and for himself, a "danteity," would be a confused product of the fancy, dear to the anarchic
individualism of decadents but unknown to
serious thought. And when thought goes in
search of an external unity beyond the process
involved in particular forms, little by little and
without being aware of it, it places one of these
forms ahead of the others or allows it to dominate the others. This tendency is to be found

in various attempts to characterise Dante, where, for instance, we find theology or politics set above poetry, as if poetry were simply the instrument of theology or politics, or as if poetry did not really exist at all. Or it takes the form of sonorous and empty phraseology, as when it is said that in Dante there is not the theologian and the poet, the politician and the philosopher, the simple narrator and the allegorist, but all these personages in one. Or it is said that in the " Comedy " are to be found all literary and non-literary styles, and all spiritual forms, the drama and the epic, the treatise and prophecy, and so forth. Certainly in this way, all is unified, but rather by force of words than by virtue of thought. It is not the nature of true thinking to embrace everything confusedly.

Another rather common objection is connected with the foregoing. It is said that taking the poetry of Dante apart from the allegories, doctrines, and erudition contained in it, we fall into disagreement with the author, who wished it to be viewed and judged according to the æsthetic theory he had inherited from the Middle Ages. But it would seem useless to repeat a thing which should henceforth be con-

sidered evident, namely that Dante the poet is
not the same thing as Dante the critic, and that
the acts of poetic creation and of philosophic reflection upon it are two distinct and different
acts, and that it is therefore necessary to treat
the poetry of Dante, not according to Dante,
but according to truth, in the same way, for that
matter, as we treat Plato and Aristotle, not
according to their own philosophy, but according to what is the new truth of philosophy, and
Homer, not according to the little-known poetic
theories of his contemporaries, but according
to the eternal principles of poetry. If we
wished to do otherwise, and to think Aristotle
with the thought of Aristotle, and Dante with
the thought of Dante, we should find ourselves
desperately engaged in an impossible effort to
distort our own mind, which certainly remakes
and rethinks antiquity, but only in so far as it
supersedes it. To say that in reading Dante
in theological company we get into closer corre-
spondence with Dante's own will in the matter,
is to say a thing not open to doubt; but in
the present case, it is not a question of a will
to interpret, but of poetry. To say, as has often
been said (and I read it again in an American
book), that Dante would burn with disdain for

his greatest admirers and critics of the present day, for De Sanctis and Symonds, who were only affected by the sensible and poetical beauty of his work, is not an argument against, but rather in favour of a criticism which has covered a long distance from the days of Dante to our own. The æsthetic and the criticism which he practised in the ways then possible, were his affair; what we practise should be our affair.

But what is to be the æsthetic criterion we are to follow? If criticism in general has progressed, and with it the criticism of Dante, from the Middle Ages through the age of Romanticism to that of Idealism, can we still accept to-day the criterion that was formed in the last of these periods? It was certainly and without doubt superior to that of the neo-classic period. Notwithstanding that it brought much of the past in its train, it was able to place poetry at the summit of things in the world of the spirit, and Dante in the world of poetry. It could set him up as a perfect poetic genius and no longer as a teacher of doctrines, exhorter to virtue, or learned man of lètters. Yet its æsthetic interpretation never succeeded in touching the right point, when determining the nature of art. It oscillated without arriving at a definition between the two extremes of a symbolical and a strongly realistic representation of the Idea or Cosmos.

Among certain critics, especially Italian, the first extreme prevailed. In poetry, and in Dante, they celebrated loftiness of concept and high morality shown in solemn and splendid forms. But this was not the more modern, the richer or more weighty of the two tendencies. Romantic criticism inclined to the other extreme, owing to the influence of contemporary currents opposed to the old classicist, didactic, oratorical, and rhetorical literature. It set great store by passion. Now passion is without doubt the very stuff of poetry and of art in general, and without passion poetry and art do not appear. But the romantics often confounded, on the one hand, passion as " material," with passion as " form," thus lowering the ideality of art, and on the other hand conceived passion as material in a restricted and arbitrary sense. They believed, for instance, that they could not find true passion outside certain confused, agitated, or violent forms and tones of passion, shot through with flashes of illumination serving only to deepen gloom and add exasperation to fury. They believed that this ideal was attained in the plays of Shakespeare and in certain of Goethe's characters, such as Werther, Faust, Mephistopheles, and Margaret, and in the poems and plays of Byron and of lesser writers. The result was that other tones and forms of passion, such for example as those expressive of security of thought, calm firmness of will, moderated energy, virtue, faith, and the like, were held to be less poetical or altogether unpoetical because they were (in the opinion of these critics) without conflict, that is to say, conflict in the sense above described. The result also followed, unconnected with the former, but nevertheless psychologically explainable and proved true by the later fusion of Romanticism in Verism, that a tendency sprang up to conceive of art as a reproduction of reality, of a reality that is itself arbitrarily limited, gross, tangible, and strident.

The proper criticism of Dante's poetry has been obscured in several places by these æsthetic preconceptions and predilections of the Romantics. If they did not invent, they at least gave nourishment and vigour to the common belief that the poem of the " Inferno " is poetically superior to the other two, since it is that in which the human passions find their place, whereas they lose somewhat of their force and relief in the " Purgatorio " and vanish away altogether in the " Paradiso." In the " Inferno," too, we find concreteness and poetry and in the " Paradiso " only an insipid spectacle of beatitude. To this can be added the other judgment that the great poetic characters are to be met with in the first half of the " Inferno " and that we gradually descend to less dramatic sinners, until we reach " prose." To these critics, also, is due the condemnation of the doctrinal parts of the " Comedy " as prose in verse or as didacticism. To them also (I mention only the principal errors), is traceable the affirmation that Dante was well equipped to describe Hell, for which he was easily able to find a model in earthly life, but was bound to fail in the representation of Paradise without the aid of observation and experience. Schopenhauer among others repeated this statement, in order to obtain from it confirmation of his pessimistic judgment of the world, which was perfectly capable of being represented in an Inferno, but never in a Paradiso; and Leopardi had already remarked something similar in his " Zibaldone."

What little of truth some of these judgments

contain will be seen in the proper places, but it
is quite certain that they contain a great deal
more of falsity, and that arguments about how
much is false and true in them are generally in
support of untenable theories. Take the theory,
for instance, of the arbitrary restriction of the
sphere of the passions, or that of the representa-
bility of Hell but not of Paradise. Truly, as
regards the latter, Dante knew what his critics
do not know or have forgotten, that Hell, Purgatory and Paradise, all modes of life beyond
the grave, are neither representable nor con-
ceivable by man. He intended only to give
symbolical or allegorical representations. Constant and eternal torment surpasses the capacity
of the human mind no less than constant and
eternal joy. They are both unthinkable, because both are contradictory and absurd. But
setting this aside, and assuming that all these
three kingdoms are to be found somewhere on
earth, they would nevertheless always be an
external reality, the object or rather the work
of naturalistic observation and of the classify-
ing intellect, and unattainable for art, which
draws not things but sentiments, or rather,
creates its lofty imagery upon the sentiments.
Not to speak of Paradise, it is impossible to

draw artistically a rose or a cloud if imagination does not first transform sentiment into
either rose or cloud.

With this statement we have already fore-
shadowed the criticism which is to take the place
of the idealistic and romantic æsthetic, and
which is in certain respects its correction and
refutation. It embodies the conception of art
as lyric or as lyrical intuition, a speculative conception to be kept distinct from the empirical
conception of lyricism. During the disputes as
to what literary class the " Divine Comedy "
belongs to, the dramatic, the didactic, or a mixture of all, the " lyrical " has sometimes been
suggested. But the lyricism of which we speak
is not a kind of poetry; it is poetry itself; it is
every work of art, whether it be called painting, architecture, sculpture, or music. It has
nothing to do with the immediate outflow of
feeling, and in the case of Dante with the expression of his " subjectivity," his character, or
practical personality, as others have asserted
and attempted to prove. It is an idea introduced by the new criticism to solve the antitheses that burdened the idealistic and romantic
æsthetic. This rightly desired to seek a sub-

stance for art, but ended by finding it in external reality and in a new sort of " imitation of nature." It was right in seeking a theoretic form, but ended by finding it in a symbol, or sensible presentation of a speculative concept, thought or half-thought. The new criticism attempts to solve these antitheses by taking practical sentiment as material and by the elevation of sentiment to intuition as form, or to the rank of a theoretic problem which art both sets itself and solves with the creation of the image. The blame that has been put upon it for having reduced art to the echoing of passion, and for promoting ultra-Romanticism, is undeserved and does not require refutation, for it is evident that only by this new synthesis can the old antithesis between romantic and classic be overcome. It can further be shown that the use made to-day of the words " lyrical," " lyricism," " lyricity," by artists lacking both order and harmony, is the romantic caricature and perversion of a non-romantic conception, which originally appeared as a correction of Romanticism.

The methodological principles which I have been explaining are not confined to the study of

Dante alone. They clearly extend to every kind of poetry and art. But they are those which it is most useful to bear in mind when attempting to remove the chief difficulties in which the criticism of Dante has been and is still involved.

CHAPTER II

THE YOUNG DANTE AND THE DANTE OF THE COMEDY

The poetry of Dante is principally, it might almost be said solely, the poetry of the " Divine Comedy," for there he at once attained to complete originality and artistic excellence.

In making this statement, my intention is not to depreciate the " Vita Nuova," the love verses, and the other poems contained in the Canzoniere, but only to make clear what a superstitious and undiscriminating admiration is apt to conceal, that in his early poetry Dante is moving with the themes and tendencies common to the literature of his time, which he does not greatly alter or subvert by the introduction of anything new and original. He is lovingly occupied with details, and only here and there brings in an idea of his own, or an image that is wholly fresh and direct. What is marvellous in this? Dante, too, was young once and cultivated the literature of youth; Dante, too, sought his way, and Dante, too, may have thought he had found it and rejoiced in the fact, when in reality he had only followed an agreeable footpath or byway, which did not lead to his appointed goal.

At first he allied himself with a literary school that had been recently founded in Italy, the School of Love, which is one with the cult of the " gentle heart," by which woman was raised to the rank of a celestial personage, a messenger of God, an angel, an ambassador and a promise of Paradise, shunning base desires, envy, and hate, and inspiring noble and virtuous feelings. Dante soon assumed the leadership of this school, advancing and perfecting its common object. In it he recognised Guinicelli as master, sage, and father, and he found himself in company with other young men who burned with a like flame. The title with which he chose to honour the work of this school in remembrance of his youthful triumphs still survives— the " sweet new style." Their ideal had been formed by refining and elevating the old erotic ideology of the poets of Provence and the Italians who imitated the Provençal style and were also apparently inspired by scholastic philosophy and Christian and Franciscan mysticism. This does not mean that their ideal possessed on this account intrinsic poetic merit, which never belongs to " schools "; for schools are formed by a consensus of opinion upon certain ideas and purposes, by certain mental and practical tendencies based upon external forms, and they always retain what may be described as a more or less intellectualistic character. Poets who attach themselves to these schools and delude themselves into believing that they follow them, always break away from them when they have become true poets by doing something at variance with the programme which they have accepted and professed; or they respect the school only in external and secondary matters. True followers, who really carry out the programme and are faithful in their attempts to obey it to the letter, are thus led to introduce an element of " will " into their artistic work, to a greater or less degree, according to the range of their poetical powers and the maturity of their intelligence.

And Dante was, in general, a faithful scholar in his youth and had his woman-angel, to whom he gave the name of Beatrice, in token of his own assumption of the literary throne. It has been disputed, and it is still disputed, whether

Beatrice was a real personage—a Florentine
girl whom he had really met and loved, or an
ideal creation, who embodied the experience and
memory of various loves, or whether she was
merely a figment of the poet's imagination.
This question would be without any weight
whatever and would deserve to be put with
many others of the same sort which are asked
about all poets, and which have more or less
importance for biography but are of no value
in a discussion of poetry, if another question of
more genuine literary interest were not bound
up with it. The question is simply this: Is
Beatrice an artificial image, a cold intellectual
creation of thought, or does she possess poetic
warmth and reality? And this question leads
to another: What is the æsthetic value of the
love poetry of Dante? In a way, we have already answered both these questions in assert-
ing that Dante's early poetry is the poetry of
a school, and that for this reason Beatrice, at
least in certain respects, is poetically unreal.

The writings of the youthful Dante—and
not only the earliest in the old style, but also
the poems that follow the ode which he describes as the true beginning of his new style
("Ladies that have intelligence in Love"),

and the others that are not included in the " Vita
Nuova "—might be called the products of a
cult, the performance of rites, ceremonies, liturgical plays, in which love and the other emotions of the soul are personified, and the woman-
angel behaves in this or that manner towards
her lover, who has around him, in his sufferings
and his achievements, compassionate and helpful spectators of both sexes. Hence the
marvellous effects that she produces upon him
who loves her and upon everyone else. Praises
of the " Gentilissima " are poured forth. The
poet trembles at the sight of her, he adores, he
weeps, he seeks pity or pardon. With such
postures of the cult of courtliness or religion
nothing is possible but eloquence and the colours
of rhetoric. The soul has placed itself poetically
in a false position, which is, however, not false
from the practical point of view, in so far as it
is the deliberate realisation of the school's
programme and of what pleases its faithful
adherents and wins their approval and enthusiasm.

But rhetoric, also, has its degrees and its
forms; and the rhetoric of Dante (and of some
of his friends and contemporaries) is not that
mechanical, tiresome, and repugnant rhetoric

which shows itself especially among mere *littérateurs* and imitators, and in the last phases of the life of a school. It is a young man's rhetoric. The woman-angel is the figment of the mind, but side by side with it there moves the vague youthful dream of beauty, virtue, suavity, purity: a most audacious dream in its flight through the heaven of the beautiful and the sublime. And all this is not thought, but affection, aspiration, sighing, exaltation—in short, something spontaneous and sincere. This passion does not create its own form; but it takes one that already exists and therefore does not quite fit, being too spacious, too architectural and conventional. Yet it permeates and animates this form with life and emotion.

Intellectual concentration is incarnated in a young woman, the " colour of pearl," with an ecstatic smile—a figure which one sees and does not see, vague, fugitive. The sense of beatitude that she sheds around her is ineffable; he who does not feel, cannot understand it. And this young woman who shows so little of herself, beyond the charm that she diffuses, has had her history created for her. Hers is the history of angelical apparitions; for as a being that has nothing to do or to love upon earth, she soon dies, or rather passes away. Admiration for this most beautiful, most divine apparition; grief at her disappearance; regret that she is no longer upon earth, although she is in heaven and in the heart of him who has loved her; the dominion that, dead and far away, she yet has over him, and the mode of life and feeling which she imposes upon him—all render beautiful and immortal this poetry of a school, which the poet consecrates to Beatrice.

Affectionate words, delicate images, are sprinkled throughout. Take, for instance, the description of those beautiful eyes which bring the lover to the lady's feet: " how level, suave and sweet they rose upon me! " or the description of the young women whom the poet addresses, their faces radiant with beauty, and minds " vanquished and pensive for love; " or of Beatrice who " smiles a little; " or of the coming of the two girl friends " laughing in each word," Monna Vanna and Monna Bice, " one marvel after the other; " or the description of that " colour of love and pity " in the face of the lady who looks so compassionately upon the lover mourning the death of Beatrice; or of the " gentle thought that insinuates itself into the heart of him who has already loved and argues so sweetly as to make his heart agree." Take, also, the representation of death, of a death that is at once torture and a renewal of tender- ness,—the anguished word that is heard as though with senses stunned, and which the lips repeat incredulously: " Thy lady is dead that was so beautiful; " and the way the reality of death is made clear in the pious offices of the friends or relations who " cover " Beatrice with " a veil," thus separating her from a world to which she no longer belongs; the gradual dis- solving of the torture in humility and in the desire for death, which is " henceforth some- thing gentle " because his lady has received it to herself; and again the calling upon and the lamentation for the dead: " Beatrice, and art thou really dead? "; and the comfort which the poet feels in hearing her name: " and as I call, upon her, I feel comforted," as if she were alive, again.

Linked with these stray words and images, is an exquisiteness of rhythm and sound, found also in Dante's youthful lyrics, almost to be called music. It is the music of a ravished soul, wrapping conventional forms and figures of speech in its own harmonious flow. This is Dante's " new style." It is truly " inspired by love;" and the two sonnets: "My lady carries Love in her eyes" and "So gentle and so virtuous she seems," may serve as instances of its sweetness. Such devices as Dante uses had been used by other rhymers, but Dante caresses and refines them in such a way that although he may say what others have said before, something is set free from his verses that goes beyond the significance of words. Certain beginnings of other compositions of his ring persistently in the ears, such as "All my thoughts speak of love . . . ;" "Like to a fair and newborn babe;" "For a garland that once I saw all flowers will make me sigh . . . ;" and certain turns of phrase and rhythm: "Whoso sees me and loves me not will never know Love . . . ;" "How often soever I saw her again I always found in her new beauty . . . ;" and the like, in great number. The opening of one of Dante's ballads, "Ah, cloudlet that in shadow of Love . . . ," though lacking clear sense or distinct image, as first published, yet was found by Carducci to be so pleasing and so popular that he included it in one of his odes.

There is, however, something of incompleteness in this supersession of sense by sound, in this poetic talent, which does not draw its par-

ticular determinations from itself, but takes
them from literature and surrounds them with
harmony; and certain verses might not without
reason be looked upon as deceptive. The two
sonnets and the other compositions quoted above
are something like the butterfly of the Goethean
apologue, which, when closely examined, lost its
various changing hues, and retained only a
languid blue; they show themselves to be efforts
of style, composed of general or vague set
phrases, of repetitions and of a little padding.
The poetic inspiration has not been sufficient to
give them a solid body. Sometimes the beginning is promising, but does not sustain itself in
the course of development, and soon declines, as
in the sonnet of the travellers and in that en-
titled: " Guido, I should wish. . . . " The latter is large in its fine original impetus, but not
happy in its somewhat expeditious and prosaic
execution. It pleases more, as one might remark, for the idea than for itself; for the
nostalgia that it suggests than for the picture
that it paints. Indeed, the texture of all this
work is generally somewhat simplicist. This
may be observed, even in the ode to Death, the
most beautiful in the " Vita Nuova," where is
to be found a little scene representing women

surrounding a sick man, very much in the style
of Giotto and reminiscent of certain of his fres-
coes. The ode does not separate and elevate
the properly poetic motive, the anguished dream
of the beloved woman's death, but puts it on
the same plane as the circumstances of sleep and
waking, and develops it in the same way as an
anecdote. To announce the death, it uses an
image of the end of the world and a flight to
Paradise during which little angels drive before
them a white cloudlet and sing hosannas. The
image certainly produces an effect but a rather
facile one and is certainly not in keeping with
the intimate trembling accent of the underlying
motif which rings out in the last strophe. There
is greater compactness than this in some of the
ballads, tenuous, epigrammatical, madrigalesque
or sententious as they may be, and in such trifles
in rhyme as the sonnets sent to the poet's friend
Cino. For instance, take the sonnet about hunt-
ing, or the one about Alisetta or Lisetta, who
runs " boldly " along the accustomed way of
beauty, sure of the conquest she is about to
make, but finds the " tower " of the mind firmly
closed against her, and another woman sitting
there as Lady; the fair one hearing herself dismissed with all courtesy (thus gracefully it

ends), "all covered with shame, withdraws."

The verses of the young Dante, therefore, are not "stupidities," as some have dared to call them. Nor is there any necessity for defending them by futile contentions: such as that they represent the transition from the old lyric poetry to the poetry of Petrarch; or that the arguments say the opposite of what they wish to say; or that the lyrics of Dante belong to a mode of feeling no longer ours and therefore do not speak to the soul. They do address themselves to our feelings in their own way and in certain passages, as a writer's early work always does, even though it belongs to a school, if he is a born poet. But we must certainly drop the exaggerated and false admiration of these poems of Dante's due to the new-style, pre-raphaelite vogue of the nineteenth century, and the craving for mystical raptures and sublimities. We must, on the contrary, look at them simply and truly, as we have suggested above.

Affectation should be still more completely banished from the consideration of the little book in which Dante made a selection from his poems, framing them in a prose narrative and accompanying them with a commentary. It appears that one cannot now pronounce even the

name of the " Vita Nuova " but the heart pal-
pitates with a mysterious gladness, full of sighs
—which is supposed to distinguish the souls of
the elect from those of the common herd. Subtle
critics have investigated the nature of the work,
to determine whether it be a sort of auto-
biographical chronicle, or the history of a soul,
or an allegory of moral truth, or a love romance
told in sonnets, odes, and ballads linked with
prose—or all these things together in certain
proportions, unified in a certain way. It has
also been said of it as of the " Divine Comedy,"
that it is a book without a peer, unique of its
kind, individual and indefinable. In reality, the
" Vita Nuova " is written like a little book of
devotion, with clearly pious intent and in an
appropriate style. Dante composed it in
memory of a special saint of his own—the
woman-angel Beatrice, whom he had sung, and
the thought of whom was to serve as his guide
among the toils and accidents of this earthly
life. It is impossible to say what autobiographi-
cal foundation it possesses, because in every case
realistic or historical details are mingled with
imagery, and this makes them all imagery.

Furthermore, whatever the truth of the matter, it makes no difference to the nature of the

little book; for if Dante had hypothetically endowed an ideal of his imagination with a history also drawn from his imagination, simulating reality as his ideal simulated a woman's personality, the character of the book would remain the same. Real or imaginary, the incidents narrated (for example, the defence, the refusal of the salutation, the various dreams, the jest, the death, the second falling in love) serve to enforce the poignancy, the exaltation, and the adoration. To the procedure proper to a book of devotion are to be attributed the talking in enigmas, the indication of astronomical correspondences, the symbols of colours and numbers; and the tone of such books—their exaggeration, their pretentiousness, their pious unction—is by no means out of harmony with the exaggeration, the pretentiousness, and the pious unction of the "new style." Were the search not desperate here, we should advise handing over to biographers the question of what moved Dante to compose the work: whether it was his wish to erect a monument to a dead woman whom he had loved, and to his first youth that had closed; or whether it was not rather the desire to give unity and a higher meaning to certain poems sporadically written, around which he had woven the elements of a fictitious narrative in order to preserve them better and more worthily; or, again, the need of a beacon in his journey through life, which should always mark his port, recalling, idealising, or imaging a fount of beatitude enjoyed and not altogether lost, which he might find again some day and be united with (as he afterwards represented in the " Divine Comedy ") ; or finally, all these different purposes combined. But if this doubt excites the reader's curiosity and leaves him perplexed as to what is real and what is imaginary, it does not increase the poetical value of the work, unless of course it is held that confusion, lack of aim, and vagueness, are attributes of art and, in the words of romantic rhetoricians, transport us into a state of dream or drowsiness. But the " Vita Nuova " impresses us as a thing of artificiality and even pedantry rather than of dreams; take for instance the many explanations in prose which attempt to analyse grammatically the various poetical compositions and to convert them into little tales.

Poetically, what remains of the " Vita Nuova " beyond the principal part—the lyrical element which we have already described and

criticised—are certain narrative qualities, certain words, certain flashes. For instance, Dante
draws the portrait of the man who has a sweet
secret and is unwilling that others—vulgar and
gossiping folk—should cast their eyes upon it;
the spirit enjoys, the body suffers, and those who
see him thus absorbed and consumed, ask him
what can have thus destroyed him; and he
" smiling looked at them and said nothing." He
tells us also how the thought arose in him of
using another woman to conceal the fact that
he was thinking of Beatrice : one day, at church,
there sat between him and the lady of his
thoughts " a gentle lady of very pleasing aspect,
who looked many times upon him, marvelling at
his gaze, which seemed to have her for its
object," and since many noticed this gazing
and gossiped about it, he thought that he would
take advantage of their gossip. And he describes the purifying effect of beauty, of virtue,
of joy, when he says that at the appearance of
Beatrice " no enemy remained to him; indeed,
a flame of charity came over him, which caused
him to pardon whomsoever had done him an injury." Elsewhere comes in the first poetical motive, as it seizes hold of the poet's soul—not an
abstract concept, but already word, beginning,

verse, and at the same time quiver of voluptuous delight and joyous salutation: " Then I say
that my tongue spoke as though by its own impulse, and said, ' Ladies that have intelligence
in Love.' These words I joyfully bore in
mind." Towards the end we read the episode
of the pious lady, in which narrative prose vies
with intercalated sonnets.

We have not sought to discover whether some
or all the component parts and narratives that
we have mentioned, and the " Vita Nuova " as
a whole, are allegorical; because, allegory or
not, allegorised *ante* or *post festum,* their poetic
value and significance, or lack of it, remain the
same. For instance, the ballad: " Like to a
fair and newborn babe," is not essentially different, whether it be referred to a real woman or
to the science of Rhetoric, which is held to be
its subject according to the interpretation now
in vogue. It is evident that when abstract
Rhetoric is thus impersonated, the imagination
is irresistibly led to celebrate her in her personified, and not her abstract form. Nor does the
question of allegory affect the nature of the
" Pietra," which may be called an ode of sensual
exasperation. The lady is unwilling to yield
herself, and the lover in his vain passionate ex-

citement imagines that he seizes her by her
blond tresses and does with her " what the bear
does when it frolics." The art of the poem is
unchanged even though certain authoritative interpretations hold " Pietra " to be Florence.
But if we suppose, for the sake of argument,
that Dante so intended and thus purposely selected the image of a hopeless love, we should
find that this image, with its attendant memories,
hopes and fancies, had substituted itself for the
original thought and that, *currente rota,* something altogether different had resulted from that
which originally *coepit institui.*

For the same reason, there is no special group
of allegories to be recognised in the book of
Dante's songs, not even those which he expressly
considered allegorical—those containing the
allusions he unveiled or proposed to unveil in
the " Convivio." However allegorical they had
been or became, they are nevertheless what he
calls them, " sweet rhymes of love." These are
substantially like the poems collected in the
" Vita Nuova " and like others which he allowed
to go uncollected. They are to be looked upon
as love poems. That they have not, as a matter of fact, great strength or beauty as such, is
not because of any allegory in them. It is be-

cause they are empty and cold and creations of
a mind hesitating between two inspirations.
Thus, when we read the ode: " You who move
the third heaven with your understanding," in
whatever sense we take it, whether as the representation of a struggle between a new and an
old love, or as between love of the religious life
and love of philosophy, it is unconvincing, because the struggle itself, and the second love
which strives to supplant the first, and the remorse which follows, are not described with living emotion, but are petrified with the over-
intellectual and conventional forms of the
" new " lyricism.   The ode, " Love which
reasons with me in my mind," goes to enormous
lengths in praise of the lady. It says that Love
tells the poet things which he cannot tell again:
that the sun sees nothing more sweet than his
lady; that every celestial intelligence gazes upon
her; that God inspires her with his virtue; that
the divine virtue shines in her and makes people
love her; that she makes the beauty of every
woman; that her beauties, since they descend
from heaven, are unspeakable; that she inspires
humility, conquers wickedness, and was thought
of by God when he created the world—and the
like. But it does not contain a living word, a

concrete image, to express emotion. Of course, such a sonnet as " Two ladies at the summit of my mind," is not to be considered as an allegory. The two ladies are Beauty and Virtue. They dispute as to the different love that they cause and decide that the one can be loved for pleasure and the other for " lofty doing." But in this case all we have is the picture of a soul attracted by two different affections and finding ultimate satisfaction in the thought of eclectic conciliation.

The didactic group is, on the contrary, to be held distinct. Dante himself closely defined its limits. In the best known of his didactic odes, he declares his abandonment of the " sweet rhymes of love " which he " was wont " to practise, the " customary speech," the " suave style," and states that he relies " upon the hard and meagre verse," to do him good service in confuting " the false, vile judgment of his adversaries." These poems are really prose in verse. The verse exists merely as a decoration and mnemonic instrument. For example: " He who defines man as an animated tree, firstly says what is not true, and secondly does not say what is entirely false; " " When I say that all virtue comes chiefly from a single root, I mean that virtue makes man happy in his work." In others of these poems, the didactic element is expressed rather rhetorically and satirically, as we see, for instance, in the themes beginning "Afterwards when love which is concerned with true and false gracefulness," and "It causes me grief." This last is directed against avarice, which renders unworthy the love of gentle lady: "Tell me, what hast thou done, thou blind avaricious misdeed? Answer me, if thou canst say other than nothing. Cursed be thy cradle that flattered such dreams in vain."

In the compositions known as the poems of the "Pietra" we come to love poetry very differently coloured from that for the ideal lady—poetry full of sensual ardour and violence. Tyrannous passion is here effectively drawn: "I cannot fly from her but she comes back to my imagination, even as the thought that brings her there. The crazy soul which draws inspiration from evil itself, boasting her own beauty and cruelty, thus makes and depicts her own punishment. Then it looks upon her...." The ode "Thus in my speech" is particularly emphatic, where we find the same image of the poet's not being able to liberate himself from the fascinating tormenting vision, which is yet

so beautiful—" As flower on stem, thus she occupies the summit of my mind; " and he begins
to talk wildly of the wayward lady's unexpectedly falling in love with him, of his even-
tually having her entirely in his control, of sati-
ating himself and bestowing upon her " peace
with love." But the form is not pure and un-
alloyed, for the poetical quality is in part rendered superficial and in part disturbed by the
virtuosity of the figures and rhymes, to such an
extent that some philologists have even compared these poems to exercises in style and
metre in the Provençal manner.

The interplay of rhymes is the most striking
thing in the ode " Love thou sawest " and in the
sestina on the short day. Antitheses, comparisons and long drawn out metaphors abound in
" I am come to the edge of the wheel," and in
the ode already quoted which opens with
the wish to be as hard in speech as Pietra is
beautiful in fact, the wish finding its fulfilment
in a style full of warlike images, of arrows,
bows, swords, shields, deadly assassins, and
thieves. Nevertheless, poetry flourishes in the
most artificial of the sestinas, as we see in the
three initial verses which portray the loss of
colour in the country at the on-coming of winter.

" I have come tired to the short day and the great circle of shadow and to the whitening of the hills, when the colour in the grass is gone. . . . " There are the verses beautifully describing the birth of spring: " The fair weather that warms the hills and makes them turn to green from white, covering them with little flowers and with grass." True poetry appears in certain delicate images and sayings: " When she wears a garland of grasses upon her head, mingling the yellow of her curls with the green, she drives every other woman from our thoughts; she is so beautiful that Love comes to stand in her shadow. . . . " And there are one or two trembling sonnets, such as that which begins " If the sight of her beauty were not taken from me . . ." in which the exile sees in love the balsam that would render his misfortune light and endurable and the bitterness of his wounds in the absence of his lady less hard to bear.

Just as in these poems of the " Pietra " we pass from the chiefly rhetorical attitude of the " new style " to a certain humanity of passion and emotion, so in certain others the ethical feeling of the poet frees itself from rhetoric and at the same time abandons the nudity of didacticism. A fine sonnet ("If thou seest mine

eyes "), is attributed to Dante, but its historical
origin is open to various conjectures. It is an
aspiration for justice, a-quiver with horror for
the evil which the poet sees around him and for
the fear that it strikes into the heart of the
faithful. The poem rises to the level of a
prayer that justice may be done: " But thou,
fire of love, light of heaven, raise her up clad in
thy veil, this virtue that lies naked and cold, for
without her there is no more peace upon earth."
The greatest of this ethical group, on the other
hand, is without doubt Dante's own work.
(There has been doubt expressed, but without
foundation.) We mean the " Ode to the Three
Ladies." As we have already remarked, it is
useless to seek the allegorical foundations for
this poem. They have been lost—the actual
names of all the three women and the true reason for their coming from the sources of the
Nile. This time the poet rightly warns us, as he
takes leave at the end of the ode: " Let the
obvious portions suffice." And indeed they do
suffice. The three ladies, sorrowful and down-
cast, like banished folk, go dishevelled and bare-
foot, with torn garments; they are received into
the poet's heart as into the house of a friend.
They are in themselves images of virtue, of

purity, of heartfelt sympathy, of dignity; three beautiful, majestic and sorrowful women, like three goddesses. The poet feels himself in his vision to be in their presence; he feels as keenly as they the injustice from which they have suffered, and the bitterness of exile and poverty, for these ladies are of the same blood as he, and belong to the same lofty society—the aristocracy of virtue and misfortune.

If we now glance backward from the "Divine Comedy" upon these poems, and in its light ask what are their relations to it, we shall have to admit that they are few and slight. It is commonly admitted that the "Vita Nuova" forms the introduction or entrance to the "Comedy," a sort of prologue upon earth to the drama of the world beyond; yet although the thought of describing the vision of the world beyond is announced at the close of that little book, and although Beatrice reappears in the "Divine Comedy," all this does not constitute a poetic relation, or affinity of tone, between the two works, but only a material relation, due to actual circumstance or theoretical premise, a figure or rather a name that passes from the early to the later work. There is no longer anything of the "new style" in the "Comedy."

Dante certainly harks back to it, but as an historical fact, a boast of his youth, as the form of his first appearance in the world of letters, with the applause that met him there. The didactic poetry of the odes is still more remote from the doctrinal poetry to be found in certain parts of the " Comedy " and especially in the third canto, where the inspiration is deeper and the tone altogether different. It may be said that in the first case there is didacticism and not poetry and in the second that the poetry absorbs the didactic element: in the first case the adjective negates the substantive, in the second the substantive dominates and determines the adjective.

There is a rather closer affinity between the " Divine Comedy " and the passionate and ethical poems; and certain lines, such as " What high honour is to be acquired in taking vengeance," " The exile that has been accorded to me I hold to be an honour," " To fall with the gods is nevertheless worthy of praise," sound almost like parts of the " Divine Comedy ": they are nearly, but not exactly, in its manner. Dante completed his artistic education in the minor poems. This must generally be admitted, especially if we understand education to consist not only in the development of certain qualities, but also in the getting rid of certain others by trying them and finding them to be fallacious or by wearing them out in some other way. Dante displays great mastery in his lyrics, and when we contemplate them we should perhaps correct the judgment of a critic to whom it seemed that in them, " Italy already had her poet, but not yet her artist." The reverse is rather the case, for in them Dante the artist or artificer was already formed, but not yet Dante the poet.

The prose works—the " De Monarchia," the " Convivio," certain parts of the " De Vulgari Eloquentia " and of the Epistles—are more closely connected than the lyrics with Dante the future poet; but here, too, the connection consists chiefly of material, that is to say, of intellectual interests, of moral and political ideals, of hates and loves that were later transfused into the " Divine Comedy." Sometimes that ardour and admiration and fury which we find repeated with a more sublime accent in the poem shines forth in the prose; for example, the exaltation of imperial Rome in the " De Monarchia " and in the " Convivio," and particularly in the " Convivio " the love of philosophising, the enjoyment of argument, the invectives, the complaints, the enthusiasm for virtue, the ferocious propensities (as in the phrase which has become celebrated, of answering "with the knife"), and the dignity with which the poet speaks of himself and of his exile. The prose of these treatises, so robust and virile, so passionate yet so restrained, very different from the lamentations and the rather affected style of the "Vita Nuova," reveals to us a new Dante, or rather another and a new aspect of Dante's soul and genius.

Yet though we may be able to observe in other artists or thinkers the process of preparation for their masterpiece, this is not the case with Dante. His minor works do not represent the beginning of the future synthesis, nor do they even reveal all the scattered elements of which it was to be made up, or even the chief among these. Other documents from which this formative principle could be deduced are wanting—those belonging to the years in which the planning and writing of the great poem made him "lean." The antecedents of the "Divine Comedy" will be found rather in the general spiritual and intellectual conditions in Italy at the time of Dante than in the minor works of the poet. To understand the "Comedy" we must therefore place ourselves imaginatively in the last period of the Middle Ages, when modern civilisation was developing in all its forms, although the mediæval conception of the world had not yet been superseded. Philosophy was still the same, although penetrated here and there by certain claims of experience and of the logic of experience, so far as this was possible. Political doctrine remained shut in between the Church and the Empire, although some assertion had been made of the autonomy of the state, that is of the new human Church. Criticism was under the control of authority, but this was growing less rigid and humanism was approaching. Historiography, stirred by interest in the political doings of the day, was developing through its relations to the life of the communes and other states; accounts of the beginning and end of the world were being thrown more and more into the background and almost forgotten. Secular architecture was reappearing, in forms ever more various, by the side of ecclesiastical architecture; and a sort of naturalism or new mode of human feeling was being introduced into painting. In political life, the Church, although it did not relinquish verbal assertions of supremacy, accommodated its policy to the changed situation, humiliated and enslaved as it was at this time, not by the Emperor, but by the King of France; while the communes continued their strife, becoming ever more and more democratic and approaching the crisis which led to the Signorie. At that period, the divine and the human, heaven and earth, the transcendent and the immanent, mingled, alternating with and combating one another, and attaining equilibrium, like two forces in the same field.[1]

Dante was not a simple representative and reflection of his age, as might be supposed, but rather one of its chief factors. Transcendency and immanence affirm themselves in him with equal vigour. He was constantly occupied with the thought of eternal life, and he was a close student of ecclesiastical doctrine, conceived as the firm truth upon which he could securely take his stand. At the same time, he was open to the influences of the external world and so keen a politician as to become almost ill from his addiction to politics. He scrutinised the most abstruse dogmas, but he also examined curiously

[1] On the character of this period, see my *Theory and History of Historiography,* translated by Douglas Ainslie, London, Harrap, and New York, Harcourt, 1921.

and with delight every aspect of human nature and every movement of the human soul. He composed treatises in the mediæval and universally spoken Latin, others in the new vulgar tongue, which had become very powerful both in prose and verse. He was a theologian as well as a versatile and highly sensitive poet. The two forces of the age, equally vigorous and powerful, and equally sincere, are to be considered the true background and material of the " Divine Comedy," which is far richer, more complex, and many-sided than could be inferred from the minor works.

Such was the subject-matter by which Dante was connected with his age, which, as we have said, he both expresses and constitutes. But since this subject-matter became poetry in his spirit, he goes beyond it and creates something which has no precedent outside itself. For it is never really possible to find the poetical sources of poetry; and that poetry which is sometimes said to be the source of Dante's inspiration—his early works and the literature which he knew and by which he had been influenced—is not truly poetical, as it appears to be when superficially considered, but is on the same level as all the other historical elements which

entered into the "Divine Comedy." Dante
created a new "tonality" in poetry, in which
the various forces and tendencies, both his own
and those of his age, were united and fused,
resolving themselves into the eternally human.

CHAPTER III

THE STRUCTURE AND POETRY OF THE COMEDY

The sentiment of worldly things was united very strongly in the soul of Dante with his firm faith in the world beyond the grave; " heaven and earth " both had a hand in his poem. Consequently the representation of the other world, of Hell, Purgatory, and Paradise, was not the intrinsic subject of his poem, its generative or dominant motive. A representation of this sort would have required an absolute predominance of the belief in the transcendent over the immanent, a disposition proper to the mystic or ascetic, who hates the world. It would have taken a nature fierce and hard, or ecstatic and devotional, of which it is possible to find some poetic examples in Christian hymnography, or in certain odes of Fra Jacopone. The rhythm would in that case have been greatly accelerated, the images flowery and evanescent, energetic in some places, vague and dissolving in others, as in the expression of aspiration and terror, characteristic of those who feel the immediate presence of God.   It has been said of Dante's "Paradiso," that it should not have been developed as a detailed description, but condensed into a single winged lyric expressive of aspiration for I know not what of divine and intangible, a saying which could be applied equally well to the "Inferno," changing, of course, aspiration into horror or terror, and to the "Purgatorio," changing it into a mixture of fear and hope, of distress and joy.   But Dante, when he composed the "Divine Comedy," was not in this narrow condition of spirit, but in one far more varied and complex.   Upon the real world, in his emotional imagination, the other world did not superimpose itself, but on the contrary formed part of one single world with it, the world of his spiritual interest.   Here both had a share, the real world perhaps a larger share than the other, certainly not a smaller one, so that the other could not in any sense overcome, or enslave it.

Those who set out to enjoy and pass judgment on the "Divine Comedy" without first recognising that its poetic subject or motive is not the representation of the other world, conse-

quently become involved in difficulties and contradictions. The same is true of those who hold
the variant opinion that the subject of the poem
is " this world looked at from the other world."
It is clear that no mystic or ascetic can
ever abolish the world. He can only deny
its real existence, looking down upon it from
the altitude of the other world as upon an
inferior stage above which he has climbed.
Such a way of looking at the world, however, involves losing sight of the colour in
human things, and argues a lack of interest
in them, and indifference towards particular
affections and actions, and towards individuals as such, who are looked upon in general as elect or reprobate, whatever may have
been their characters, their works, their passions, their virtues or their earthly greatness.
But there is nothing of all this in Dante. His
emotion has a hundred channels and not merely
the single one of veneration for the elect and
disgust for the reprobate. His judgment is not
confined to the legal or divine judgment " he is
saved " or " he is damned," but becomes
widened into a moral judgment and discerns the
good in the damned, the evil in the saved. Sometimes he allows free course to loves and hates,

sympathies and antipathies, and treats shadows
as though they were substantial things, and
spirits who have been judged and have definite
situations in the other world as though they
were many-sided men with full vital faculties, a
fact which leads those who accept the above
definition to say that Dante went into the other
world carrying with him all the passions of this
world. But it is precisely in this manner that
it is impossible to go into the other world
(poetically at least). To go there requires that
one should divest oneself of human passions and
look upon things with new eyes, with the eyes
of one who has awakened from an anxious and
ugly dream and finds himself amid true and radiant reality. So that the definition of the subject of the poem as " this world looked at from
the other world " is not only incorrect, but im-
plies that Dante has been illogical, that he has
done the very opposite of what he meant to do
—as though he had really performed some action and had not simply poetised. Of course,
he could not be illogical in poetising a sentiment
so various and complex, or in poetising any sentiment whatever, since sentiment is never either
logical or illogical. It was simply his system of
thought that was illogical, that is to say, in a

certain sense not entirely harmonious, thus resembling that of any man or of any philosopher. Every system has a side which is not entirely harmonious and logical; and it is from this side that the new thought issues which is called progressive.

Positive as well as negative criticism confirms me here. For instance, the philosopher in Dante is " mediæval " and the poet " modern " (the first, that is to say, ascetic and mystical in his plan, the second passionate and political in his execution). Confirmation also appears in the fortunes of the " Comedy "—particularly the discontent which mystic and imaginative spirits have more than once evinced towards the poem's presentation of the other world. It has seemed to them too definite in outline, too calm, with too little of Hell in the " Inferno," too little Paradise in the " Paradiso," and too little Purgatory in the " Purgatorio." Too little effort seemed expended on redemption. Again, direct confirmation is afforded by the kind of impression every one gets from reading the " Divine Comedy," or by the memories retained from previous readings. Certainly it is not the image of the other world that remains; it is not the terrifying perdition of the " Inferno," the labours inspired with hope and with suffering of the " Purgatorio," nor yet the felicity of the " Paradiso." The final, synthetic image, which sums up all the impressions made by the poem in its different parts is the image of a robust will, of a heart that has experienced much, of an intellect sure of itself, in short, the image of Dante himself. His personality dominates the many different personages of the poems, whether they be of vigorous temperament and ardent passions, of violent and truculent attitude, or of mild and gentle senses and serene mind. It stands out above the landscapes, now grim and scorched, now fresh and delicious, now dark with shadows, now swimming in light. It dominates the scenes resonant with pitiful or lofty words, weighty with advice and instruction, or scornful, irate, solemn. The image of a robust will, of a heart that has experienced much, of an intellect sure of itself, the image of Dante, dominates the whole. The author of an eighteenth century study of the " Comedy " was therefore not so far wrong when he proposed to substitute the " Danteid " for the usual title of the " Divine Comedy."

We experience no feeling of repulsion for the

damned in the " Inferno " but rather, for many
of them, familiarity, tenderness, affection, reverence. On their side, they evince great solicitude
as to their fame, as though they were merely
condemned to earthly exile. They are careful
to correct unjust and evil judgments current
about them: " infamy torments them more than
the pains of hell." Sometimes they happen to
jest or almost to jest; at any rate they converse
with calmness, exchanging information and
reflections. Friar Catalano, that sad hypocrite
walking beneath his cowl of lead, remarks with
perfect good nature to Virgil when the latter
realises that he has been deceived by the
demons: " I heard of the many vices of the
Devil when I was at Bologna and among them
that he was a liar and the father of lies." So
even one of the damned had to have known Bologna and its university in order to suspect how
devilish the devil can be! Virgil also jests,
when, addressing a question to the forger afflicted with the itch and furiously scratching
himself with his nails, he adds ironically, " If thy
nails last thee eternally for their present purpose." Beatrice in Paradise laughs when she
hears Dante addressing Cacciaguida with reverent restraint as " you " rather than " thou."

" Laughing, she seemed as though she were the one who coughed at the first fault of Guinevere ": as malicious and satirical as the lady of Malehaut at the first declaration of love which Launcelot and Guinevere make to one another in the romance.

Doubtless Dante does not lose the inner consciousness that he is in the other world, that he is walking round the blind kingdom, the infernal abyss, among the atrocities of damnation, and from time to time he gives vent to such exclamations as this: " How great is the power of God that rains down such blows for vengeance ! " " Oh ! most miscreate of all denizens of the place whereof speech is difficult, you had been less abject as sheep or goats ! " Or he affirms that the different plagues had " made his eyes drunken, so that they were desirous of continuing to weep," and that he still is sad whenever he " remembers." In the " Paradiso," when he stands before the Rose of the Blessed, he tries to signify the immense force with which the spectacle affected him; to show how it swept him off his feet, he has recourse to the amazement that fell upon the barbarians of the north when they saw Rome and its multitudes of edifices and monuments. " I who came to the divine from the human, to the eternal from time, to the just and sane from Florence, with what stupor must I not have been filled?" But it cannot fail of notice that this translation to the divine is stated rather than represented, and that the exclamations of terror to which the poet gives vent sound a little as if suggested rather by the thought of the infernal punishments than by the actual feeling of them. For this reason they seem somewhat cold, especially if we compare them with the emotion that finds its way into the heart and continues to increase irresistibly in the presence of Francesca. A Frenchman and Catholic wrote a little volume in which he set himself to answer the following question: " Did Dante return a better man from the other world?" He answers the question in the negative, taking into consideration the poet's tenderness for seductive sins, his lack of compunction for his own faults, and the fact that the only fault which seems to bother him there at all is the omission of a " vendetta." Although he accomplishes the formulas of penitence with a very good grace in Purgatory, he thinks a great deal more of earthly than of heavenly things, and shows himself to be rather an observer full of curiosity than a penitent. In

Paradise, he is a sort of student at a good series of lectures. Thus under the guise of a capricious psychological examination is reached the same conclusion as our own, namely, that the other world is not the dominating poetic motive in the " Divine Comedy."

On the other hand, it must be admitted that Dante intended precisely to represent the other world. Indeed it was probably the original idea and intention of the poem to do so; and this is not merely a matter of argument, but can be confirmed from several passages in the " Vita Nuova." It is also evident that he imagined a certain form for the three kingdoms. Hell was an abyss, extending from beneath Mount Sion to the centre of the earth, and including variously within its nine circles, rivers, woods, sandy wastes, precipices, castles and ruins. Purgatory was a very lofty mountain rising from a small island at the antipodes of Mount Sion. It had a rocky base (ante-Purgatory) seven mountain ledges, and a forest which was once the earthly Paradise. Paradise was imagined as extending through the nine spheres of Moon, Mercury, Venus, Sun, Mars, Jove, Saturn, stars, and crystalline or *primum mobile*. It also extended into the empyrean where God

was, the " unmoved mover." Dante divided the
damned, the penitent and the blessed into their
various classes and allocated them to their respective circles, ledges of mountain-side or
heavens. In Hell, he placed the lazy in the
vestibule, and those who had been redeemed
from original sin, in Limbo. The truly damned
were placed in pits in the other circles according
to the three kinds of sinful disposition, incontinence, violence, and fraud, each one of these
divided in such a way that the path led downward from the luxurious, the greedy, the
avaricious, to the traitors, lowest of all. In
Purgatory, the contumacious and the negligent
are assigned to the base of the mountain, or to
ante-Purgatory, and all the others to its ledges,
according to the division of the seven sins or
capital vices. In Paradise the blessed are arranged according to their merit and respective
beatitude, and according to their various degrees of charity or of cardinal and theological
virtues. Finally, in order to describe this triple
kingdom, Dante imagined himself as a traveller
and an observer. At first, he was under the
guidance of Virgil, then for a short time of
Virgil and of Statius together. From the earthly
Paradise upwards to the empyrean, Beatrice

was his guide, and in the empyrean, Saint Bernard.

What was Dante actually doing in making this picture, which is certainly to be found in the " Comedy " and serves indeed as a foundation for all the rest? He was not, properly speaking, composing poetry, since the necessary and creative motive is lacking. Nor can we invoke science, because science, in all the forms that it assumes, whether it elaborates concepts, or constructs abstractions, is always critical, and does not admit, indeed drives away and dissolves the combinations of the imagination. Here on the contrary the imagination appears as a demiurge and accomplishes a work that is altogether practical, shadowing forth an idea of the other world for its own use. This work of Dante's might perhaps be correctly called a " theological " or an " ethico-politico-theological " romance, by analogy with " scientific " or " socialistic " romances of recent times. Such romances are still written, with the object of divulging and rendering desirable and acceptable to others something believed or desired by the author, and presenting it with the help of the imagination. Such *desiderata* nowadays would be the effects to be produced by

certain expected and hoped-for scientific discoveries, or new conditions of life to arise from
the realisation of certain social changes. With
the alteration in historical conditions and the
interests of men, now that the natural and
sociological sciences have become what theology
and the problem of the soul's salvation once
were, theological romances are no longer composed; but there were many composed during
the Middle Ages (among which are to be num-
bered what are called "visions") and this
romance of Dante was by far the richest of them
all, the most grandiose and the best constructed,
although not the last. It was a theological
romance in which the dominant influence of religion and the political and ethical utopian
interests of Dante were inextricably mingled.

It is quite evident that Dante, with a theological romance in view, was bound to take pains
to give precision and cohesion to his imagery,
to make it what is called life-like, and this was
further facilitated by the introduction of the
miraculous, in which both he and his readers
believed. He was so successful in this that the
legend arose that he had really visited both Hell
and Purgatory, and that Paradise had, at least
in ecstasy, been revealed to him. The ancient

commentators were obliged to insist again and
again that he was writing as " a poet " and not
as an historian, and even moderns who do not
need this warning, often express astonishment
at the marks of reality which Dante confers
upon his narrative. But that the meticulous
explanations which he gives as to the configura-
tion of places and the mode of travelling, as to
the time occupied by the journey and as to the
phenomena observed, or that the dissertations
with which he explains and justifies these
imaginary things, treating them as though they
were real and the confirmation of some scientific
theory—that these explanations and dissertations prove that he was himself deceived by
his imaginings and fell into a sort of hallucina-
tion, is on no account to be admitted, however
variously it has been maintained. An over-
great dose of madness would be thus introduced
into the genius of Dante, causing us to lose
some of the respect we owe him. Such an hy-
pothesis is quite at variance with the lucidity and
self-consciousness of his mind. But more than
that, it is unnecessary. All composers of
theological, scientific or socialistic romances
are precise in their statements and meticulous
in their reasoning about their imaginations.

Their undertaking demands that they should be so.

One of the most conspicuous sections of Dantean literature has been devoted to the structure of the " Comedy." It vies in bulk with that which has accumulated about the allegories and is called " physical topography " and " moral topography " of the three kingdoms. Since Dante desired and achieved that topographical construction which we find in his book, it is natural that the interpreters should occupy themselves with and explain it. It is also useful, in order that readers may get the landscape clearly in mind, that maps should be made of it. As a rule, readers have but a summary and confused idea of it. That there should be geographies of the Dantean world, horaria giving the times occupied in the journey, and commentaries upon the penal code and upon the scale of merits and rewards, is inevitable and useful. But the advice already given must here be repeated with emphasis, namely, to beware of exaggeration and to remember that these constructions of Dante's are merely imaginary and for us at any rate of but little importance. We have other visions than these in our heads, and in any case it is not well to be a bore, " wearying

others," as Monsignor della Casa said in the
" Galateo." It is certainly a loss of time and
very wearisome to listen to a discussion as to
whether Dante spent seven, eight, or nine days
on his journey, and twenty-eight or forty-two
or seventy-two hours in Paradise, at what precise time he made the ascent, whether before or
after midday, and the like. But the Danteists
compel us to make another more serious stricture at this point, a stricture which concerns
their lack of method. Let us explain what we
mean. Although Dante was minute and meticulous in his procedure, he has nevertheless left
lacunas in the texture of his theological romance,
and however attentive he was, he has here and
there fallen into contradictions. This may be,
as some think, because he was not able to give
final touches, or even a general revision to a
poem which had taken several years to compose under the influence of many various events.
Had his work been of a philosophical and critical nature, it would have been possible to fill
the lacunas and solve the contradictions, as we
do when studying the philosophers, resuming
and continuing our enquiries after each gap and
drawing the logical consequences from the
author's propositions. But since the " Divine

Comedy " is a work of the imagination and
what Dante has not included in it also belongs
to a realm of the imagination, it is not possible
to supplement him logically or to reconcile the
parts which contain contradictions.   We may,
of course, continue to employ the imagination,
without Dante's good reasons for doing so. But
this is to indulge ourselves in dreams. Danteists
do not as a rule recognise this process when
they see it. Behold them (to give but a couple
of instances) discussing as to how Dante passed
from one to the other bank of Acheron; or to
what place the souls of children and those of
virtuous pagans in Limbo will go after the last
judgment, and whether a site in the " divine
forest " will not be assigned to them as a per-
manent abode. How, they ask, can Cato possibly be the guardian of Purgatory, seeing that
he died half a century before the incarnation of
Christ? Purgatory did not yet exist, so that it
must be presumed he went to Limbo during the
interval, and was taken from there. But in that
case, another difficulty arises. Cato, in the
" Comedy," does not know Virgil, yet Virgil
was in Limbo; we must suppose, therefore, that
there were various circles or clubs in Limbo, and
that Virgil and Cato did not belong to the same

one. Or, it may be, that during the ages which
had passed since he had assumed the office of
guardian of Purgatory, Cato had forgotten the
speech and gestures of his former companion.
Then there is the question whether we can believe Cato is to be saved, or whether after the
last judgment, " he is to return unwillingly to
Limbo," or will on the contrary proceed to
heaven and there find a suitable abode. And so
on with other so-called Dantesque questions,
solved in like manner, and about which it will
be polite to say nothing.

What is worse is that zealous researchers
into the physical and moral topography of the
three kingdoms presume that the answering of
such questions assists the understanding and the
enjoyment of Dante's art. They believe it
really helps us to understand the character of
each of the three cantos with its various parts
and episodes. Hence they regard the " history " of the other world as an " æsthetic history " and the linking together and the devices
adopted by the poet a refinement of art. But
since the structure that we have briefly delineated arises from a didactic and practical
rather than poetic motive, research does not
serve either to indicate the particular poetical

character, assuming that there is one, of each canto, or the passage from one poetical situation to another, but can yield only what is in its nature to yield, namely, things which are external to the poetry and determined by structural connections. Every effort made to convert structural reasons into artistic reasons is a sterile waste of intelligence. The poetry of the three cantos cannot be deduced from the conception of the journey through the three kingdoms by means of which humanity, and Dante who represents it, is supposed to pass from anguish and remorse, to repentance and purgation, and from that to moral beatitude and perfection. This is one of the aspects of the theological romance, but it is not the formative principle of the poetry adherent to it. The very beautiful representation of the Venetian arsenal does not find its function and poetical justification in the supposed intention of Dante to oppose a spectacle of fervent economic activity to that of the swindlers' wicked work, which is the material of the canto. Nor have the excursus of Virgil on the origin of Mantua, and the idea of giving an example of a trustworthy story among the inventions of the witches and the magicians, and Ulysses' narration of his

last heroic voyage of exploration, anything to
do with the fraudulent among whom Dante
finds himself condemned.   Each one of these
episodes stands by itself and is a lyric by itself.
Nor can the structure that supports the poetry
be considered as the "technical part" of the
poem, since technique (as must henceforth be
admitted) either does not exist in art or coincides with art itself, whereas the structure of
the "Comedy" since it has a practical origin,
does not entirely coincide with its poetry.
With greater truth this structure has been
compared to a frame which surrounds and contains one or more pictures.   Such an image,
however, runs the risk of again bestowing upon
the structure a properly æsthetic virtue, since
a frame is generally thought of together with
a picture, or as artistically carved so as to form
a harmony, almost a complement to the picture, and this is certainly not the case in the
present instance.   Comparison for comparison,
the structure of the "Comedy" might rather
be figured as a robust original framework upon
which a luxuriant vegetation is clambering,
decorating it with pendulous boughs, festoons
and flowers, and so covering it up that only
here and there does some wall-space show its

rawness, or some angle its hard line. But dropping simile, its relation with poetry is simply that which exists between a theological or didactic romance, and the lyric which continually varies and interrupts it. This relation is to be found in other poetical works and above all in the " Faust " of Goethe. " Faust " has certainly been compared with the " Comedy " on historical grounds (such as that the one is the sum of mediæval thought and the other of that of modern times). But a glimpse of their artistic similarity has also been a cause of comparison between two works, so different in many ways, an artistic similarity which is rather external, lying between their conceptual or didactic characteristics.[1]

There is no denying that theological romance does have a repressive effect on poetical inspiration. We may observe this effect in frequent instances. There is the necessity for the insertion of parts that are merely informative, or of certain symbols to which no particular keys are afforded. Coherence has to be sacrificed and personages and scenes, which have an emotional value of their own, forced to serve as expedients for the imparting of certain infor-

[1] See my Essay on Faust for further analysis (Bari, 1919).

mation or for the explanation of certain doctrines. Farinata for instance abandons his
disdainful attitude and forsakes the thoughts in
which he is absorbed, and which are all of them
patriotic and political, in order to explain the
limits of the knowledge of the present and the
future among the damned. Virgil and Dante
himself, as he is represented in the poem, are
obliged to lend themselves to all the necessities
and sinuosities of the narrative, with the result
that their respective characters lose their homo-
geneity. This can be seen when they are taken
alone, apart from the poem; at the end
Virgil is no longer the same Virgil who was
sent by the heavenly ladies, nor Dante the sinner
who set out on the path of purification, so docile
and so contrite. The poet must also contend
with repetition of similar situations, and we
find him trying hard to vary them, without being
altogether able to overcome their monotony.
As instance of this, we may select the astonishment of the souls in Purgatory when they perceive that Dante throws a shadow, and the explanations that Virgil is obliged to supply from
time to time. At a certain point, he himself
appears to become impatient with it and to act
like the man in the old story who had a stain of

oil upon his clothes and was so informed by every one he met. Finally, whenever he met any one, he said at once: "Yes, I know, I have an oil-stain." So, too, Virgil says, "Without your asking, I confess to you that what you behold is a human body, by which the light of the sun upon earth is broken." And finally, not to dwell too long upon this kind of thing, the somewhat sudden and decided manner in which scenes and dialogues are concluded is due to the same cause. It has been jestingly said that the characters of Dante leave one another without ceremony, that they take "French leave," or more seriously that Dante "brands a mark" upon the forehead of his characters and passes on; and it must be confessed that owing to the necessity of keeping to the scheme adopted (the "curb of art"), his Hell is a little crowded or choked, and his Paradise so expanded as to seem rather empty by comparison.

But we must also remember the freedom that this ultramundane and encyclopædic scheme permits to the imagination of Dante. It has a beneficial influence also in another direction. Owing to it the poetry of Dante assumes a sort of necessary character, bursting its way through the barriers and rendered more vigorous by the opposition. It tops all obstructions in such a way that one could not offer a better case to the unbelievers in the real, autonomous existence of poetry, who look upon it as something artificial and unessential. We would have them reflect on this poetical fury of Dante, the theologian and politician, this torrent that flows in so lofty a vein, opening its way between the boulders and tearing impetuously along. Such is its force, such its richness, that as it penetrates into all the hollows of the rocks and covers the mountain landscape with spray and foam, it often leaves nothing to the sight but the motion of its own waters. The poetry of Dante, when it can do nothing else, vivifies the argumentative and informative and technical parts of the narrative, even the not infrequently laboured conceits of the erudite historian, and invests all with its own accent, emotional and sublime.

For this reason, scheme and poetry, theological and lyrical romance, are not separable in the work of Dante, any more than the parts of his soul are separable from one another. One conditions the other and flows into it. In this dialectical sense, the "Comedy" is certainly a unity. But he who has eyes and ears for poetry always discerns in the course of the poem what is structural and what is poetic, a distinction sharper here than in the work of other poets, in which the like may be found, but in equal measure perhaps only in Goethe's " Faust." Almost a complete contrast is presented by the greater part of Shakespeare's plays where scheme or structure is born of poetic motive and there is not structure and poetry, but all may be called homogeneous, all is poetry.

A somewhat rhetorical admiration is often bestowed upon the " architecture " of the " Comedy," its sureness of line, its proportions, its " eurythmia," the mathematical correspondences to be found in the construction of the three kingdoms and in their physical and moral topography. This is a favourite subject for lecturers, who are led to talk ornately of the " æsthetic beauty " of the poem's structure, a sort of beauty additional to the other beauty of the poetry, a beauty of " the thing in itself," as it is sometimes called. Thus a recent Italian poet and student of Dante succeeded both in breaking up and impoverishing the poetry of the " Comedy " by finding it only in the " non-dramatic parts," in certain " pearls," fished up from that great sea, and in exalting the

" poetry of the conception itself," the " most
poetic conception that ever was or will be in the
world," the journey beyond the world. To
this there is nothing to be said, save that there
does not exist a poetry of things, but only a
poetry of poetry, and that to talk of the poetry
of things can in the most favourable case be only
to use a graceful figure of speech; it is certainly
not to use a critical way of thinking. The
structure of the " Comedy " is also admiringly
compared to that of the Gothic cathedrals, with
the curious result that a comparison first employed in the eighteenth century to express contempt of Dante's work as rough, extravagant,
barbaric and " gothic," is now used for just the
contrary purpose. To this result of romantic
mediævalism and religiosity, we must reply that
cathedrals are cathedrals and not the schemes
of poems, but poems themselves; that the
Gothic cathedrals expressed a new mode of
feeling, arising from a new conception of the
divine and the relation of God and man, heaven
and earth; and that Dante too expressed a new
mode of feeling in his poetry but not in any abstract plan. It might perhaps be possible to
employ the comparison, but in a very different
sense, were Gothic architecture to be considered,

not at the moment of its origin and full flower, but during its decline, or rather its change in the time of Dante, and if we were to look upon it as the effect of spiritual changes like those which we have spoken of as acting upon his soul. Then the picturesque sculptures and decorations, which in the original Gothic were not independent, artistic wholes in themselves, but rather architectonic parts determined and inspired by the spirit of the edifice, began to obtain relief and importance for themselves, and the churches took on a new and more worldly aspect foretelling the Renaissance.[1]

Thus it seems clear how the structural parts of the " Comedy " should be treated and how much attention should be paid to them. They should not be treated as pure poetry, nor rejected as unsuccessful poetry, but rather respected as practical necessities, while we go in search of poetry elsewhere. They should be respected, despite those Danteists who fix a curious and indiscreet eye upon them and end consciously or unconsciously in joking about them, talking of the " enforced domicile " of

[1] The recent monograph by M. Dvorak, to be found in the *Historische Zeitschrift* (1918, vol. 119), *Idealismus und Naturalismus in den gotischen Skulptur und Malerei,* is very instructive on this point.

Virgil, of the "alpinism" of Dante and the
like.   But we should not insist upon them;
our attention should dwell elsewhere, that is to
say, we should read Dante just as all ingenuous
readers do and are right in doing, paying little
heed to the other world, very little to the moral
divisions, none at all to the allegories, and
greatly enjoying the poetic representations, in
which all the poet's multiform passion is condensed, purified and expressed.   It may, and
will be said that much of Dante is thus lost.
But the opposite is true; we obtain even more of
him, the contemplation of him as a supreme poet
is increased in intensity.   It may be and has been
said also, that Dante is thus profaned, his religious thought being abstracted.   But neither
is this true.   Only those thoughts whether
political or religious, or whatever else they may
be, are removed, or rather set aside, which have
not been translated by him into his poetry.   On
the other hand, in the poetry lives much serious
and sincere religious feeling, even where it does
not seem to be directly expressed; it lives in all
the most striking portraitures, because it also
lived in the soul of Dante, even if reconciled
with or balanced against other sentiments.
Finally it will be, and has been said that thus

all unity is denied to the poetry of Dante. But this is even less true, for unity is wrongly sought outside the poetry, in a concept or practical scheme, and all the old and new disputes as to unity of thought and unity of action in the poem are idle, like that as to whether the protagonist be Dante himself or not, and so on. The true unity of his poetry is the poetic spirit of Dante, of the Dante of the " Comedy," not the Dante of all his works; and the shortest and best method of determining what is this spirit in its distinguishing features, is that of running through the three divisions of the " Comedy " with especial heed to the principal lyrics or groups of lyrics which they contain, and to differences of inspiration and treatment.

CHAPTER IV

THE INFERNO

The poetry of Dante does not rise at once to its height; it begins simply and becomes gradually more and more copious and varied, more free in motion. A strong and sure crescendo extends from the first cantos to those of the middle and end of the " Inferno," and thence more quietly through the " Purgatorio " into the thin air of the " Paradiso." The first cantos of the " Inferno " are the slightest, either because they formed part of a first sketch, touched up and added to (according to a respectable tradition and well-founded conjectures), or because they shared in the uncertainty common to all beginnings, increased in this case by the difficulty of constructing and setting in motion the great machine.

The first canto especially gives the sensation of effort, with that " midst of the pathway of life," where we find ourselves in a wood that is

not a wood and see a hill that is not a hill, and
gaze upon a sun that is not the sun, and meet
three wild animals that are and are not
wild animals, of which the most menacing is
thin, owing to the desires that devour it, and, we
do not know how, " makes many people live
in woe." The imagination tries to satisfy itself
with the representation of a road, of a danger,
of succour, but no sooner is it moved and excited than it is driven to a different representation, this time of a soul-history. Expressed in
images, as we find it in the work of other artists, this may be beautiful too. But here the
imagination is driven away from it because the
history is rather confused than made clear by
the images employed. Connecting links are
weak, both here and in the following cantos. Informative replies are introduced through hesitating and provocative questions, but there are
many questions that are unnecessary as well as
answers that go beyond the point. Thus Virgil
asks Beatrice why she does not fear to descend
from heaven to Limbo, and Beatrice in reply
utters an aphorism upon the things that we
should not fear and tells him that she cannot be
touched by infernal misery. The representations are summary and the style itself, the

rhythm of the terzina, has little body and is often prosaic.

But the words addressed by Dante to Virgil in the first canto are already trembling with emotion, when he sees the ancient poet before him and hears him speak, the poet who for so long a time had formed part of his inner life, the master of wisdom, the master of " the beautiful style," so distant in time, so near to all his thoughts. The second canto, too, is resplendent with the happiest strokes, though here too the informative intention manifests itself and there is a tendency to oscillation in the allegory. The heart of Dante believes in the blessed ladies who are watching and guarding him from yonder skies. The first of these is she whom he loved so deeply in his youth and by whose aid he emerged from the vulgar throng. His youthful dreams clustered about her person, her name illuminated his poetry: Beatrice. Beatrice is now the eternal feminine, she is piety; hers is an almost maternal solicitude, yet with something in it of the soft and amorous. She is a saint, but a beautiful woman always, and in a manner belongs to him alone who celebrated her alive and dead. The other ladies, friends of Beatrice in the court of heaven, are not ignorant of this ancient tie. They are careful to warn her of the danger which menaces her faithful lover, divining her desire and anticipating her will. She departs and goes to Virgil and persuades him, speaking to him " with an angelic voice, soft and low," with delicate flatteries and gentle promises of gratitude, concluding her discourse with the supreme and irresistible feminine argument of tears. " Her eyes she turns away shining with tears. . . ." To express the fluctuations in his soul, the poet here uses the image of " flowerets " bowed and drooping beneath the nocturnal frost, now warmed in the rays of the rising sun; they " rise up all open upon their stems," and thus resemble him who has reached the shore and looks back upon the ocean which he has traversed—an image of terror overpast which Dante has elsewhere employed.

The entrance to the Inferno, in accordance with the plan of the poem, is by a gate bearing an announcement partly explanatory and partly terrifying. The moralist begins to exercise his judgment and to graduate the sins and vices of mankind. He places the lazy, the timid, the perpetually irresolute, unfit for good or evil, almost outside of this graduation, according to

a fantastic law of retribution. Contempt en-
velops them, and their true punishment is in the
verses which score them forever: " These
wretches, who never were alive "; " Who lived
without infamy and without praise . . .";
" Displeasing to God and to his enemies . . .";
" Who made through cowardice the great refusal . . ."; " Let us not speak of them, but
look and pass on. . . ."

A great river next becomes visible and Dante
sees people thronging its banks to pass over.
A similar scene depicted by his teacher, Virgil,
comes back to the memory of the poet, and he
gives a new version of it in a manner between
the classical and the mediæval. He takes a
figure from the pagan mythology and turns him
into a demon of the Christian Inferno, the
ferocious old slave-driver Charon, with flaming
eyes and hairy, hoary cheeks, imperious, inexorable, implacable. Herds of desperate
wretches are subject to his nod and suffer from
his blows. It is an imitation of an artist by an
artist, but an imitation that replunges the model
in the reality of the imagination and brings it
forth renewed and refreshed.

The moralist and indeed the theologian
begins again with the descent, where are found

those who did not receive baptism and did not
know the true God. They do not suffer external torments, but a pain that is altogether internal, and waste themselves away in perpetual
desire without the light of hope. This is a
contradiction of human ethical feeling, a mystery of the divine justice, which Dante does not
closely scrutinise and against which he exhibits
no feeling of revolt. Virgil, who is among the
rejected, becomes deathly pale, and Dante's
heart beats, for he realises that these were
" people of great value." But the situation is
not further probed; there is scarcely an indication of the line upon which it might have been
developed and we must remain content with the
mere statement of fact. The poetry of the
passage shows an equal restraint. A similar
dry judgment appears in the scene in the noble
castle among the great and wise, at the sight of
whom the poet is said to rejoice; admiration,
reverence, melancholy, are alluded to, but not
represented. Dante will later acquire a very
different degree of liberty of movement in this
other world which he has imagined. At present
it appears oppressed by a rule of theological
law. Certain images shine out, here and there
an expression assumes a lofty tone: " His aspect

was neither sad nor glad " . . . " With slow
and heavy eyes," " They spake seldom, with
soft voices," " At that sight I exulted within
myself. . . ." But catalogues of names are
everywhere, hardly varied with an epithet.
Even when the poet finds himself received by
the master of the loftier song (Homer or Virgil) as a sixth along with the five greatest poets
of all time, he does not find adequate images
and sentiments; he says that they do him
" honour " and that among them they spoke of
things as to which " it is as well to be silent here
as it was well to speak of them there," showing by the words themselves and their turn of
expression that he has not much to say, or does
not yet know how to say freely what he would.
The vein is still running slow or is clogged.

It is not until we reach the next circle that,
in the terzina consecrated to pity for the tragic
love of Francesca da Polenta and Paolo Mala-
testa, her brother-in-law, we find the first great
unmixed poetry of Dante. The figure of
Minos at the beginning of the canto and the
rain-squall that carries souls away, do not
escape the sphere of the graphic and descrip-
tive. Those who see in the eternal tempest
sweeping all before it, a living symbol of irre-

sistible sensual desire, have probably penetrated
the intention of the author, but have perhaps
seen more than there is to be seen in the way of
actual poetic effect. The account of the sen-
sualists, Semiramis, Dido, Cleopatra, Helen,
Achilles, Paris, Tristan, is still hardly more
than a catalogue of names, though accompanied
at times with historical allusions. But the scene
becomes animated as soon as Dante turns to
" those two who go together." Their separating themselves from their companions and
their haste to fly towards the poet when they
hear his voice, together with the simile of the
doves, show them full of the desire to pour their
sad history into a human heart. Their first
words are instinct with lively gratitude towards
him who has distinguished them from the others
and has had a feeling of compassion towards
them. A delicate sensibility dominates these
two sinners for love's sake. Their love has
been love, true and proper love, full and real;
desire, sense, soft and delicate fancies, ecstasies
of beatitude, languor, self-abandonment, perdition; neither animal degradation, nor heavenly
achievement, but humanity or human fragility,
for which everything else is forgotten, every
duty deserted. The attractiveness of bodily

form and motion, the " beautiful person," the
" smiling and desirable mouth," enchain and
conquer and still tremble in the memory. The
two are not aided in resisting, but are rather
influenced the other way by the " gentle heart,"
the " sweet thoughts," the " soft sighs," the
maxims of the doctrine of love, and all the
idealisations introduced by the poetry of the
troubadours and the " new style." The memory and example of the passionate and noble
heroes and heroines of the romances is but a
lure which leads them to the edge of the abyss
and thrusts them into it. Aristocratic fineness
may conflict with vicious turpitude and cowardice, but the lovers can derive no help from it,
since fineness of sentiment, or spiritual culture,
is the accomplice of passion. The enemy to be
fought is a friend, and the sin is the very sympathy which draws human creatures to one another. Neither does the thought of the man
they are betraying deter them, nor does it fill
them with either compunction or dread. He is
the " not-loved "; he has been unjustly favoured
by fate and represents the insolence of unnat-
ural power, the oppressor first, and then the
executioner. The only escape from such
temptation is flight; to indulge the desire for

one another, to cradle themselves in dream and
" longing," is to submit without alternative.
Dante, indeed, condemns the sinners, but only
as a believer, as an ethical being; he neither
condemns nor absolves them sentimentally. He
feels interested and perturbed, his eyes fill with
tears, and finally he faints with emotion.

The tragedy of passionate love, which is the
poetic meaning of the episode of Francesca,
occupies but one page of his poem, which thus
uncovers for a moment and reveals writhing in
its untameable strength an inebriation of the
senses and imagination which the poet does not
again expose to the view. Dante was too
human not to know, to feel, and to understand
such affection in a lively manner; but he was
too virile, with too many lofty thoughts and too
great a fervour for work, to remain like other
poets, fascinated and a prisoner in the circle of
Eros, invincible in battle.

Another variation of a Virgilian figure, even
more profoundly transformed than Charon and
represented with equal vigour, is the demon
Cerberus in the third circle. Dante not only
has a lively consciousness of the most varied
emotions of the human soul, but also, vigorous
as is his temperament, a most powerful sense of

what may be called "vitality" in general, immediate or animal vitality. It pleases him to embody this sense in powerful and monstrous beings, before which he himself seems to be lost in admiration, as though face to face with the powers of nature. Others are to be met with further on in the "Inferno," but among the first is this horrible Cerberus, so powerful with his great bark and three throats, his clawing, skinning and quartering, and his constant quivering with rage and insatiable greed.

Among the souls of the gluttons, beaten by the heavy rain and tortured by Cerberus, is found the Florentine Ciacco, who affords an opportunity for a political interlude, during which there is a discussion about Florence, the power and decline of the Whites, the vices which disfigure the citizens, and the great personages of the previous generation, "whose minds were directed to acting rightly." Then there is a talk with Virgil about the resurrection of the body and the increase of torture for the damned when souls put on again their earthly garments. Clear instances, these, of what we have said proceeds from the scheme of the theological or theologico-political romance, and not from the spontaneous imagination of the poet. He works upon them, of course, and elevates them, not only by splendour of word and verse, but also by poetical touches, such as that "great longing" which makes him ask at once about the fate of those whose virtue and greatness he had learned to praise and admire from a boy. But the curiosity of the reader turns chiefly to the history of the times; hence the circumstances of the life of Farinata degli Uberti, of Tegghiaio Aldobrandi, of Jacopo Rusticucci, of Mosca dei Lamberti, of Arrigo Fifanti and of Ciacco himself, are eagerly examined and it is asked who ever could have been the two "just men" who were in Florence and whom Ciacco does not name. The description of the two opposed bands of the avaricious in the fourth circle is also a mere part of the colour scheme, when they hurtle together and dispute among themselves. A thrust is made, among many that will later be delivered with a firmer wrist, against the avarice of the clergy, among whom is to be found a large number both of popes and cardinals; and since here too the poet feels that there is a certain aridity in the treatment, he tries to enliven it with a disquisition upon Fortune. He has her rebaptised in conformity

with Christian theology and calls her the Minis-
tress of God, Angelic Intelligence, one who
changes the possession of the goods of this
world according to an occult and providential
dispensation.   It is to be observed as very significant of the character of the man and of his
poetry that those who brought with them " the
smoke " of sloth are placed at the bottom of the
swamp; for they had been sad " in the sweet air
that rejoices in the sun."   According to at least
one of several various interpretations, these are
the sceptics and practical pessimists, wearied
and disgusted with life.

It seems that Dante has abandoned at the
foot of the towers of the City of Dis the first
manner with which he entered the world beyond.   Like a villager who timidly becomes a
citizen of a great city, he begins to move about
at his ease in that country which is henceforth
for him like the earth, and where he has adventures such as might befall him in travelling in
strange and inhospitable places.   One tower
signals to another and at once a bark sets out,
steered by the demon Phlegyas.   It hastens to
the two travellers, speeded on its course by the
cry of the captain who hails him whom he believes damned and whom he is preparing to

seize and carry off. But Phlegyas too is
obliged to become quiet and obey the word of
Virgil. The meeting with Filippo Argenti
takes place as they traverse the swamp. Dante
at once recognises "that strange Florentine
spirit" and not only does not pity him but
drives him away with disdain, and adds torture
and shame, expressing the wish to see him punished before him to the delight of his eyes,—a
wish which is a moment after realised, sanc-
tioned and approved by Virgil, in a lively scene
which contains all the concentrated imagery of
hate. Revenge, that ferocious unredeemed
justice, is beautiful! Such is the sentiment
which illumines the rapid scene; and the poet
does not lack a smile of satisfaction, a sort of
joy in the work of punishment, torture, and contempt, which the sacred Muses permit him to
carry out.

Now we have opposition at the gates of the
city of Dis, negotiations as with the garrison of
a hostile fortress, refusal and confusion; Virgil
is momentarily perplexed and anxiety takes hold
of Dante; he cautiously and timidly interro-
gates his guide with a view to reassuring himself; there is the menace of the Furies and of
the head of Medusa, but finally comes the

celestial messenger, preceded as if by a hurri-
cane: before him the damned flee away, and he
opens the gate without hindrance and allows the
two pilgrims to enter. Such is the new and
more complex dramatic scene beginning here,
and here developed and completed. Its allegorical meaning is different from that of the
first canto, in that it is far more emotional and
poetical, completely informing the scene and
rendering it comprehensible and clear. It is all
one with the development of the scene itself; it
is the tension experienced among difficulties
and obstacles, the confidence that approaches
lack of confidence and yet gets the better of it,
in the strife of the just against the unjust, of
virtue against iniquity, of right against force;
and it is also the arrival of succour (from without, or is it not rather from within our breasts
themselves?) of the superior power, of authority, which sustains the forces of good and is so
sure of itself and victorious by its mere presence, like the solemn messenger of heaven who
proceeds without looking about him and hardly
needs to remove " the gross air " from himself
with a slight gesture of the hand. That power,
his duty fulfilled with the bringing of succour,
returns whence he had come, to the altitude

where he abides, without uttering a word to
those whom he has helped, like a great personage whose mind embraces a wide circle and has
other cares than those of the little beings before him.

The mind of Dante is full at this moment of
his ideal journey, of images of men, of events,
of struggles going on in his city. But the
imagination no longer places before him images
of hate; the new feeling that makes his breast
expand is admiration for the great and strong
men of Florence, which is no longer the sower
of every vice, vituperated by Ciacco, but the
" noble fatherland," of which it is his joy and
boast to be a native, the fatherland that one
curses and loves, for which one suffers and of
which one is proud and which really does stand
at the apex of the soul as a sacred thing. Farinata rises up, the figure in which this sentiment
of poetical elevation expresses itself; Farinata
the magnanimous, who like a true epic hero is
completely and wholly the warrior devoted to
his cause, to his political ideal, to the city to
which he belongs and which for that reason
belongs to him; all other affection is foreign
to him. Now he makes himself superior to
the evils which surround him, holding his head

high, with a look on his face as though he had a great contempt for Hell. He is careless of human loves and sorrows, and does not deign to pay attention to Cavalcante who is close to him; nor is he in the least degree moved by his solicitude and paternal affection. His first inquiry is that of the partisan and the warrior, who takes the measure of those who approach him to see whether he is to place them among his friends or his enemies, among his followers or his adversaries. His first exclamation is a memory of fierce strife and of a double triumph; his anguish springs from fear lest the fruit of his victory prove wasted through fault of his successors; his melancholy is that of the warrior, not rejoicing in slaughter and spilt blood, but feeling himself to be the instrument of necessity; his sole justification is that above his every hate is love, that magnanimous love, which makes him defend conquered Florence with open countenance against the less elect among his companions and allies of coarser fibre, that he may save her for the future. Dante is full of reverence and admiration, yet he is Farinata's adversary at heart, a combatant against a combatant, and would have been against him in life had they been contemporaries. He utters a bitter speech or two, but leaves the last word to Farinata and places him on a pedestal of glory.

What may be called poetry of friendship is now interwoven with the heroic poetry,—a song of sorrow for friendship once fraternal but since spoilt, if not actually broken, by events and by differences of temperament and character. Guido Cavalcante should have been the companion of Dante on his great and difficult journey; he, and no other, the first of his friends, the equal of Dante in loftiness of mind. Why is he not with him? The union of the two was so natural and their separation is so surprising that the old Cavalcante, when he first sees Dante, looks for his son too. At the first words of explanation as to why he is not there, he misunderstands, believing him to be dead. He does not await the reply, which he believes to be certain, and falls overcome with anguish. But the true pathos is perhaps not so much in this outburst of paternal affection as in that "Your Guido," on the lips of Dante; Guido is no longer Dante's. Dante restores him to his father, who still loves him so passionately, so terribly.

The celebrated exposition of the punitive sys-

tem of the " Inferno," in which human faults
are graded and characterised according to
scholastic philosophy, comes next. It is dictated
by structural motives, and although certainly
possessing the merit of precise and pregnant
diction, is without that vitality of which we are
conscious in other parts of the " Comedy." The
author had to throw a sop to the readers of the
theologico-ethical romance and he does it at the
first opportunity, in order not to have to think
of it again. The dissertation is introduced by
an ingenuous artifice; it is supposed to be a way
of usefully passing the time during a brief pause
in the descent. Here and there Dante tries to
touch it with emotion; there are timely inter-
ruptions by the listener: " Thy reasoning doth
very well proceed and well distinguish. . . . ; "
" Not less than understanding doth doubting
please me."

The descending journey begins through a
deep valley, which suggests to the mind of the
poet the Italian countryside, a ravine on the
near side of Trent, which he describes as due
to an earthquake at the time of the death of
Christ. At the edge of the precipitous rock he
meets another acquaintance of the classical
world, the Minotaur. The realistic imagination

of the poet brings this monster, too, very vividly before us. He shows it to us in all its fury, like a raging bull that has received the death-thrust, and bursts its bonds, dragging itself along and plunging about. Next, at the river of blood we seem to have reached a military encampment. The two pilgrims are questioned and threatened by the officers of the guard, the Centaurs, task-masters of the damned. We feel the presence of discipline, severity, secure governance; the sound strength of the executor of justice has subdued the strength of evil and holds it firmly under him for punishment. The Centaurs, those " nimble wild beasts," are both elegant and decorous. Nessus, though over-punctilious in his trust, really does fulfil the duty of his office. Chiron is grave and meditative, he keeps his head bent upon his breast and makes use of the arrow which he holds in his hand to draw back his beard with the notch, showing his vast mouth. He talks and asks questions and gives orders when he has been clearly informed of the facts. Nessus becomes a " trustworthy guide " and courteously furnishes information both as to single individuals and as to the various orders of the damned who occupy that circle.

The Harpies and other evocations of ancient
myths follow the Centaurs, so vividly portrayed.
Here are the thorny stumps of the sombre forest with the imprisoned human souls, recalling
to mind such Italian landscapes as those dismal
spots between Cecina and Corneto. Here, too,
begins the elegy on fidelity, a fidelity slandered
and dishonoured, and brought to a desperate
death. Piero della Vigna, suicide Chancellor of
Frederick of Suabia, says not a word against
his Emperor, who had showed himself so pitiless towards him. The Emperor remains " his
master," " worthy of honour," and Piero is
faithful, even after his unjust condemnation,
even in death, even beyond the tomb. The
injured soul speaks only against the world
and its courts, against the envious who
surround, ambush, and ruin the brave and
honourable man. The tone is one of pro-
testing accusation and disdain, but the style
is moderate and ornate, almost diplomatic;
and it has several times been remarked
by the critics that this is in conformity with the
decorous personality of the Suabian Chancellor,
—he speaks, one might almost say, in the style
of one of his aulic epistles.

Scenes and passages of a dreadful nature,

representations of tormentors and tormented, which were not much in evidence in the preceding cantos, now become more and more prominent. The forest of the Harpies springs from the souls of the suicides, which fall there and sow themselves in the ground, growing like plants. This forest is, as it were, set in action and motion by means of the souls which flee through it and cling to the trees, twisting and breaking them. They are followed by dogs, which catch them up and tear them to pieces. But the poet does not permit himself to be occupied entirely with such sights; one of the souls thus tormented, after lamentations and sighs, contrives to find a moment to represent mythologically the life of incessant strife and intestine warfare in Florence, taking as the centre of its narrative, the mutilated statue of Mars, the ancient patron of the town, which used to be seen on the Ponte Vecchio.

Another horrible region is that space of dense dry sand where the air is motionless and broad flakes of fire keep sifting down " like snow on windless Alp." Capaneus appears upon this background. He also derives from classical poetry, but his strength is here more than physical; it is also spiritual energy, mad, indomitable,

obstinate will.   For this very reason, he in-
clines to some extent towards irrational displays
of brute force.   Not only on account of his
mighty body does Dante call him " great; " we
feel that there is admiration for the reply
" what I was living, that I am dead," and this
feeling is not cancelled, it is merely repressed,
by the moral-religious reproof put into the
mouth of Virgil.

The evoking of ancient stories and myths,
which sometimes springs from Dante's admiration for monstrous and enormous physical
strength, has on other occasions a different
origin.   Things that have struck the imagination of the poet dwell in his memory and are
ready to be recalled for purposes of comparison.
Instances of this are the anecdotes which refer
to Cato in the sands of Lybia and to Alexander
in the hot regions of India.   Classical memories
are mingled with biblical myth in the character
of the Ancient of Crete.   The statue of the
Ancient, composed of clay and of various
metals, stands on a mountain in that island and
weeps tears which run as rivers into Hell.   As
usual, the allegorical meaning of this fable is
disputed and it has not been found possible to
determine it with exactitude.   Is it the history

of the human race or that of the Empire? The status is in any case singularly impressive, half figure, half hieroglyph. Notwithstanding its cryptic aspect, it yet inspires sentiment and has a message for the soul, suggesting a distant history and hinting of a mysterious fate.

The meeting with ser Brunetto (so strangely brought about in this circle, where his presence is a slur) seems to some critics to be nothing in itself but a real unexpected meeting and conversation which once took place beside the Arno between the youthful Dante and the old and erudite man of letters. This may be so; it may contain a memory of the sort. But whether real or imaginary, its sense remains the same: "*You* here, ser Brunetto?" How much is contained in this surprised interrogation! It tells of long familiarity, of confidence, of affection, of compassion for the man who loved him and is now pitiably enduring torments. In him who divined and knew him when others failed to do so and when he was perhaps unknown to himself, in him who had faith in his talent, in his soul, in his star, Dante now finds as it were, support in the war that will be waged upon him by his fellow citizens. He finds in him the sympathetic echo of his disdain, of that pride in

adversity which sustains and honours him, and
of his intention to continue without stay and
without wavering upon the glorious path of his
destiny. The soul of Dante embraces the soul
of the old man, and as Brunetto has understood
his heart, still so full of the future, so he understands the heart of Brunetto, which is full only
of the past. The latter believes he still lives in
his literary work, and recommends "The
Treasure" to Dante.

Among the representations of strange torment, so strange as even to extend to the spectacle of three grave and reverend Florentine
signors throwing cartwheels under a rain of
fire—a spectacle which would be comic, were it
given a comic accent—he pursues the course of
thought begun with his meeting and conversation with Brunetto. Other famous men of ancient Florence appear, with whose stories Dante
had made himself affectionately and reverently
familiar: Guido Guerra, who did much both
with counsel and with sword, Tegghiaio Aldobrandi, Jacopo Rusticucci. With them the discourse becomes more political; and at their request Dante utters, "with face uplifted," his
cry against "the upstart people and sudden
wealth," which have changed the aspect of his

city and driven out courtesy and valour, generating arrogance and luxury in their stead.
This is the first appearance of the feeling afterwards voiced by Cacciaguida, the repugnance which the austere man, bound to tradition and discipline and to the dream of the energetic and heroic life, feels for new fashions which he does not like and therefore does not understand, seeing in them only the destruction of old habits which are dear to him. But history moves on in its great heavy car, uprooting many beautiful things and sowing new and lovely seeds, and the heart of the dreamer, faithful to the past, the imaginary past in which he places and finds himself, can only shudder and imprecate, while sentiment and the poetry born of sentiment protest against action and reality, against the utilitarian and prosaic.

Geryon swims up from the depths of the abyss. He is the greatest creation of what we have called in Dante the potent sense of immediate, sensible, organic vitality finding form in enormous and monstrous beings. Geryon is intended as an allegory of fraud, and this time the precise sense of the allegory is certain, because the author himself declares his intention; but no poetical reader would ever think of imposing the image of fraud on Geryon, or would weaken him by making such an imposition, so truly does the representation of the grandiose and repugnant monster dominate the conception and stand by itself, so closely, almost lovingly, is it studied in every part and motion. The Fraud of Ariosto was certainly fraud, a moral conception, pleasingly contained in apt imagery which it rules and dominates; it is poetry born of the intellect and limited by the intellect. Geryon is Geryon, and his proper action is not that of defrauding, but rather lies in his miraculous mode of locomotion, his slow, grave passage downward through the air with his heavy cumbrous limbs. Yet he is sure of himself and nimble in his own way. One follows him with admiring eyes and asks for nothing more. He who does not feel poetry here is in danger of never feeling any poetry at all. When Geryon has manifested his being, fulfilled his poetic function, he rapidly vanishes away, " like an arrow from the string."

The infernal abyss again borrows form and colour from country known to the poet, and the noisy fall of Phlegethon is confounded with that of the river " which resounds from the mountain above San Benedetto." Thus also the scenes among the damned are compared with earthly scenes, and the double files of pandars and seducers, moving in opposite directions, find their likeness in the double file of pilgrims going to and fro from Saint Peter's by the Bridge of Saint Angelo in the year of the Jubilee. The usurers of the seventh circle and these pandars, seducers and flatterers of the first pit of the eighth circle, are among the vilest of the sinners; they are depicted in bestial attitudes, beaten with whips and followed by the jeers of demons, plunged in excrement, with head and hands filthy. Horror and disgust invade the soul of the poet, but at the same time the moralist and satirist is busy placing here those of his contemporaries whom he judges worthy of such a place in Hell. Then Thais, the courtesan celebrated by Terence and now a "filthy and debauched maidservant," and Jason, the seducer of Medea, and Hipsyphile, are suggested by his classical reading. But at the sight of Jason, epic memories arise irresistibly and the verse again assumes a solemn tone. Jason is introduced as "that great soul who comes and seems to shed no tear for pain," and when the poet thinks of him as he was and as he now is, admiration and reverence again prevail: "How

kingly yet he seems!" Heroes, heroines, sinners, and the rest,—great was his imaginative
delight at being able to meet and come to know
them after reading of them in ancient poems
with the ingenuous faith and fresh fancy of the
Middle Ages!

At the beginning of the canto devoted to the
Simoniacs Dante remembers his " beautiful San
Giovanni " and avails himself of the occasion
to insert a protest of an altogether private
character to rectify a slander against himself.
Here we enter upon a region of oratory and
prose. Face to face with the Simoniacs, he is
face to face with that part of the ethical and
religious life of his time which more than any
other made him shudder with disgust: the
Papacy, corrupt, intriguing with secular princes,
and greedy of worldly wealth. He collects
himself for an outburst, prefacing his invective,
already on the tip of his tongue, with an ingenious invention, a refinement of vengeance
and punishment, by which the Pope is fixed head
downwards in the pit, with his legs sticking out,
and able to take part in the conversation only
by shaking them. Furthermore, he is doomed
to subside completely into the pit on the arrival
of the next similarly damned soul, who is none

other than Pope Boniface, and he believes that
Dante, who is standing by his side, is none other
than he whom he has been expecting as a sure
arrival but not so soon. Thus Dante is the
first to learn of the damnation of his great
enemy, the first to perceive the shame that will
cover him; and he rejoices in what is a sort of
spiritual vendetta. He is all deliberate voli-
tion, and proceeds not only as public prosecutor,
but as officer of justice and executioner. He is
very different from the Dante who so completely abandons himself in the passionate parts
of " Inferno," fainting before Francesca, respectful towards Farinata, affectionate with ser
Brunetto. Here the terzina and the spoken
word become the instruments of castigation and
inspire awe. He does not become convulsed
with hate, nor does he give way to anger, nor
utter sarcasms and sneers; he simply exercises
inexorable severity, giving vent to his indignation in powerful and measured speech, not forgetting the " reverence " due to the " highest
keys," and when he condemns and punishes, declaring the reason for the condemnation and
punishment.

If we are to believe the interpreters, when he
comes to the pit of the diviners and sorcerers

Dante remembers the fame enjoyed by his master Virgil during the Middle Ages. He is also supposed to have had himself in mind, since his name was mentioned by Galeazzo Visconti as a possible collaborator in an act of sorcery prepared against Pope John XXII during a certain intrigue. On behalf of himself and his gentle omniscient sage, he is supposed to have evinced a greater energy of reproof than he would otherwise have done for the black arts, and charged the representation of their punishment with darker tints. But there is nothing of this supposed protest and calculation, nor any horror for magic and witchcraft in the canto of the sorcerers and diviners. It is above all the canto of legends and of strange, mysterious characters, ancient and modern. These, too, are brought near to us by the force of Dante's imagination and examined face to face with curiosity and wonder. We see as in a flash the portentous ruin and death of Amphiaräus, swallowed up by the earth near Thebes; the prodigious change of Tiresias from man to woman; Aruns, who beheld " with unobstructed view, the stars and sea " from his cave among the mountains of Italy, white with the marble of Carrara; and Eurypylus, who claimed the initi-

ative of the Trojan War, vigorous in appearance, even in the writhings to which his punishment condemns him, making him " stretch forth
his beard from his cheek, upon his dusty
shoulders." Eurypylus was augur when a whole
country was emptied of its men for the great
war, leaving the mothers by the deserted
cradles,—an image of the desolation caused by
war, old but eternal. He and Calchas gave the
signal for the cutting of the first rope in Aulis,
and with this cutting again arises in the mind
the image of the departure of an army for war,
with its perils and glories—the whole image
symbolised in an act, both material and moral:
the die is cast, the first rope cut. We owe the
account of the origin of Mantua which follows,
to no purpose of moral or critical instruction,
but simply to a love of ancient stories and
legends. The poet evokes primitive Italy, a
land without cultivation and without inhabitants
when compared with the present. Here the
virgin Manto settled with her slaves after much
wandering, and here she practised her arts.
Here she left her body, and upon " these dead
bones " rose the city of Mantua. There is not
lacking, with all this epic and tragedy, a certain
note of almost contemporary comedy in the

anecdote of the bungler Asdente, who had recourse to the trade of diviner, but now wishes
that he had " attended instead to leather and
string." That would have been a surer trade!
As a result he is here represented as surrounded
by those poor and comical wretches, who, instead of attending to their woman's work of
needle and thread, pose as witches and sor-
ceresses and make use of herbs and waxen pup-
pets in their sorceries.

The picture of the Arsenal of Venice which
stands at the beginning of the description of the
fifth pit, has been said, even by admiring critics,
to be too lengthy for the purposes of simile and
incapable of justification (as some have
claimed) even for purposes of imaginative contrast. We ought, therefore, to observe here
that the similes of Dante are often explanatory,
like the simile in which Malebolge is compared
to a fortress with all its moats and bridges. Or
they are used as additional proof like the simile
of the old tailor peering as he threads the
needle, or that of the soldiers who come out
of Caprona after having made their peace. Still
others, however, go beyond this and are poetry
in and for themselves, small lyrics, like the
simile of the mother who awakes and finds that

the house is on fire, picks up her son and flies, indifferent to her scanty clothing, or that of the poor peasant who finds in the morning that the country is white with hoar-frost and who laments that he is not able to lead the sheep to pasture: he looks again in a little while, and finding that the sun has dissipated the frost, becomes cheerful, and taking his crook, goes forth with his flock. Such too, is the terzina in which the whole *chanson de geste* is concentrated: " After the sad defeat, when Charlemagne lost the holy war, Orlando did not make his horn to resound so terribly "—that " terribly," in which we hear the prolongation of the last desperate sound, vainly invoking succour! And such too, then, is the simile of the arsenal, the famous Arsenal of Venice. It is full of the sentiment of toil, so fervent there, of preparation. It is winter and navigation is wholly or partially suspended; time is being saved by repairing the damaged ships and by the construction of new ones. The different works are mentioned one after the other, rapidly, the effect of the labour being expressed in the rapid movement of the verse—that labour, so various and yet so concordant, so toilsome and yet so cheerful, having ever before it the happy vision of

soon ploughing the waves again securely, of
again trafficking and acquiring riches.

Dante must have thought of his personal experiences even less in the pit of the magicians,
among the swindlers boiling in molten pitch (although in the opinion of some of his interpreters
this was not the case): If he thought of
them at all, he forgot them immediately afterwards, addressing himself to his narrative. His
mind should here have been grave, but meeting
suddenly with a comic fancy, he takes a liking
to it and depicts it with care, for the love of art,
ending by arousing our laughter and laughing
himself. By what he sees and hears in the pit
of the swindlers, we are reminded of certain
pages in picaresque romances, or of certain historical accounts of plebeian tumults, in which
farce and jest suddenly become ferocious, or of
adventures among the redskins or the natives
of Africa. Rascal meets rascal, plebeian encounters plebeian, savage meets savage, when
the swindler meets the demon. The demons
have the upper hand and are clever, but so are
those in their power, and they sometimes not
only get the better of cleverness with cleverness,
but also of superior strength. How the demons

delight in tormenting! How they sneer, how they laugh and enjoy themselves at the business! The first black devil that we meet is running with a swindler on the angle of his sharp shoulder, holding him tight with a " grip on the sinews of his feet," and as he hurls him down into the pit he upbraids him and his country in mocking phrases, while the other devils echo his words and add sarcasm to sarcasm, laughter to laughter. And when they run more than a hundred prongs into him, an image of the kitchen rises naturally and appropriately to the mind. Other demons rush out upon the two pilgrims, as soon as they have discovered them, but they are stayed by Virgil's diplomacy, the authority he invokes, and the order which their leader is obliged to give them. They halt, but in doing so, seem like an irrational and un-changeable crowd, docile and indocile at the same moment; they obey and do not obey the order, so contrary is it to their nature and habits. Their leader acts in a similar manner, for he seems to respect the two travellers and assigns to them an escort, but deceives them as to the route out of pure malignity. Dante is at first apprehensive, uncertain, but as he contem-plates the strange spectacle, this feeling gives way to curiosity. Half in wonder and half in curiosity, he watches the formation of the picturesque troupe and hears the grotesque names and nicknames of those composing it and hears also with amazement the sound of the singular trumpet. When he now recalls what he saw and heard, he cannot but smile, and the smile broadens when he hears the signal for departure given by the leading devil in so new and unthought of a way. Expression here becomes serio-comic. He tells of other departures for war, of other manœuvres which he had chanced to witness upon earth, and draws a comparison between their starting signals and the " so uncouth a cornet" which he heard in Malebolge. This state of mind continues throughout the episode of Ciampolo and his stratagem of provoking a brawl among the devils in order to escape. " Reader, thou shalt hear of a new game," exclaims the poet, immersed in a spectacle so comically strange. The spectacle is plebeian and Dante laughs, but not for sympathy with plebeians, but always as himself, Dante, who throws a glance at humanity as it were almost in a state of nature, not permitting of serious indignation nor even of repugnance, but on the contrary exciting curious observation and laughter at extravagance and enormity beyond the pale of all gentle and civil custom.

With the vision of the hypocrites, proceeding slowly beneath their splendid, blazing cowls of gilded lead, we come back to ethical characterisation, ethico-religious sentiments, and to the recent history of Florence. Recollections of the previous scene, however, still hover about the poet and suggest to him the observation on the nature of devils, which he places in the mouth of the pleasure-seeking friar. Dante is truly capable of " transmuting himself in every way " in the " Comedy." A little further on we find him almost joking as he describes the way in which he climbs up " from rock to rock " supported by Virgil and remarking that it is truly not " a path for one wearing a cloak; " and then he sits down for a moment to recover his breath and permits himself to be stimulated and reproved by his companion in grave and magnificent speech (" for cushioned in down, one neither obtains fame nor risks blame. . . . " " With the soul that wins every battle "). The epigrams with which the " Comedy " is everywhere full, have sometimes a value in themselves, so wise, so virile and so sublime are they, a value greater than that of random extracts

from speech or dialogue. Thus in a few stanzas
further on, not only does Virgil assent to the
request of Dante, but adds: " For the sensible
request should be followed by its silent fulfilment." His wise leader calls Dante sharply to
himself in the " Purgatorio " and reproves him
for his distraction when he naturally turns his
head at hearing his name mentioned by one of
the souls in his immediate vicinity, concluding
his reproof with the solemn terzina: " Come
behind me and let them say what they will: be
like a strong tower which never lowers its crest
for any wind that blows." The soul of Dante
is overflowing with thoughts and with poetry,
and bursts into expressive expansion at the least
opportunity.

Vanni Fucci, upon whom he now chances, is
a sort of degraded Capaneus. At war with God
and with divine and human laws alike, he is
plunged in vice and evil passions, a man of
blood and wrath, a thief, brutalised and proud
of his own complete bestiality (" I am Vanni
Fucci, the beast, and Pistoia was my fitting
den. . . . "). He is quick to react to the speech
of Dante, colouring up for " sad shame " and
rage, and pouring forth upon the two a malig-
nant prophecy of misfortune which he crowns

with an outrage against the divinity. A hateful
personage covered with hate by Dante, yet
Vanni Fucci is not vile; he still arouses some
admiration in us, and Dante himself is reminded
of the thunderstruck Capaneus as he looks at
him. He is isolated in the thieves' pit, which is
the pit of transformations where men are seen
catching fire when bitten by the serpents and
becoming one with them, and then becoming
men again from serpents. The sense of the mysterious and prodigious does not reign in this
scene; the feeling of dread before the terrible
nature of the divine punishment is absent. The
interest is transferred from the thing, which in
itself has but little power to move the soul of
the poet, to the way the thing is said, to the
cleverness with which details and degrees are
described in parallel process, to the address
with which all the difficulties of the task are
met and vanquished. " Let Lucan be silent and
harken to what is now let fly, . . ." " Let Ovid
be silent as to Cadmus and Arethusa. . . . I do
not envy him," exclaims the poet, sensible of the
brilliant passage that he has been composing.
Here we see the joy in artistic power which,
though certainly everywhere present in the
poems of Dante, as in those of every true poet,

is with him usually fused with or balanced
against other sentiments. In these verses about
the transformations in Hell he separates himself from the poetry in a certain measure and
steps aside by himself, and for this reason the
verses have displeased those who have sought
in them what they do not contain. They will
be enjoyed as they deserve, if regarded in the
way we have pointed out.

The feeling underlying this part of the poem
is as simple and modest as that which inspires
the character of Ulysses is large and complex.
It is beyond doubt that Dante, loyal to the revealed word and to the teachings of the Church,
respectful of the limits of human knowledge,
and believing in the Christian virtues of mod-
esty and humility, would hold the audacity of
Ulysses to have been sinful. It is natural that
he should have the violator of the Pillars of
Hercules punished by a mysterious religious
force of nature executing the decrees of wrath
divine. But Dante is something more than that
which he is or knows himself to be doctrinally;
and this something more it is which leads him always to distinguish his doctrinal condemnation
of any sin from the feeling he experiences in regard to it, as well as from his judgment of the

sinner, whom he thus condemns only in one respect. This it is which opens his mind to the
greatness of Ulysses' attitude and enterprise.
Yes, that was " the mad flight "; it certainly can
have no other end than punishment and ruin, to
be caught in the whirlwind, ship and sailors hud-
dled together like toys and sent to the bottom by
the sea which closes indifferently above them.
But Ulysses, ever burning with the desire of
knowing men and the world, unrestrained either
by the sweetness of his son, by piety towards his
old sire, or love of his wife, again sets out to
sea with his faithful grey-haired companions, to
discover that part of the earthly sphere which
is unknown to him; and this Ulysses, who inspires his companions with the lofty words:
" Ye were not made to live like brutes, but to
follow virtue and knowledge," is a part of
Dante himself, that is to say, of the profound
aspirations which religious reverence and
Christian humility were able to restrain and
repress but not destroy in him. Hence we have
this figure of the Dantean Ulysses, sinful, but
sublime in his sinfulness, a tragic hero perhaps
greater than he ever was in Greek tragedy
or epic.

At the request of the condemned soul who

succeeds Ulysses, Dante gives a picture of the
conditions in the Romagna. But what a picture! Others like it, too, are to be found elsewhere in the poem, where the mind, which
began by judging and considering with the eye
of the politician, is converted into imagination,
and sees with the eye of poetry. Everything is
expressed concretely and with solid imagery;
the pedigrees, the names of the nobles, the
rivers that wash the earth, the events of which
it is the theatre, all crowd into the imagination
like living beings. He tells of the fate of each
city as though he were speaking of the sorrows
and troubles of his own daughters, and " Romagna," which binds them together, is as
though it were the first-born among them,—
" thy Romagna," Romagna, which is never
without war " in the heart of her tyrants,"
though at present she has no open war. Love
and solicitude for that part of Italy which he
knows and to which he is accustomed, lend a
warm accent to his account. Here politics
really do become poetry. In representing a
political condition of temporary stability between two periods of change, he describes
Cesena, for instance, as " she whose flank is
bathed by the Savio," and says of her that

"placed as she is 'twixt mount and plain, she lives between tyranny and freedom."

The episode of Guido de Montefeltro has not Guido for its protagonist, but Pope Boniface, "the Great Priest, may ill befall him!" the pope, whose enemies were Christian peoples and who was all burning with "the fever of his pride." Guido is his instrument and his ingenuously guilty victim, for he plays not only for his own soul, but for the souls of those on whom he is able to exercise his authority. This scene is therefore an ideally suitable companion to that we have already witnessed wherein the pope appeared as "a brand committed to the flames," awaiting his successor Boniface. Like that, it is cunningly contrived to attain its object, and there is not wanting to it something of that ingeniousness of invention which is at the same time openly calculated and malicious. Notwithstanding the seriousness of the narrative, there is an almost comical reaction at the end. That great cheat Guido, the modern Ulysses of the Romagna, who "knows all cunning and all secret ways," is grossly deceived by the unscrupulous Boniface. The cleverness is revealed in the syllogism and in the comment upon the case by the black cherub, as he clings

to his prey: " Perchance thou knewest not that
I was a logician."

The spectacle of a field of battle and
slaughter, with all the grim jokes perpetrated
there by conquering sword in its rage, or cruelty
in its furious refinement, is displayed in the
ninth pit. But the reason is not that the soul
of Dante is troubled and revolted by any
slaughter of his kind, but rather is the moral
suggestion contained in the " law of retribution " and expressed at its best in the character
of Bertram dal Bornio, who carries his own
head dangling in his hand like a lantern. This
act of his signifies that he has committed the
crime of having by his evil counsel separated
father and son. He lifts up that head of his
and approaches it to the poets, in order to discuss his affairs, in a magnificently imagined
scene arranged with perfect verisimilitude. But
the finest moments passed in this pit are those
filled with particular descriptions, as that of
the field of Ceperano, still full of bones, " where
each Apulian proved false," and that of Tag-
liacozzo, with the epic figure of old Alardo.
Then we have Mahomet sending advice to his
friend Dolcino struggling among the Alpine
snows, and find Pier da Medicina thinking

again of " the gentle plain that from Vercelli
slopes to Marcabò." The remainder is perhaps more ethical than poetical. The intimate
nature of the inspiration reappears, on the
other hand, in the sad and wayward character
of Geri del Bello, the near relation of Dante,
whose death has been unavenged. Dante was
certainly faithful to the mediæval idea of the
family vendetta, but that is not here of consequence, for we find nothing but his distress at
meeting one who has not been avenged as he expected to be. Geri awaits the vengeance to
which he believes a long and sacred tradition
gives him claim, whatever may be Dante's opinion on the matter. But Dante neither sees
nor speaks to him, though he feels that he
is close by and stops to look in the direction
where he believes that a " spirit of his own
blood is weeping." We feel that he hesitates
and does not dare to go on looking for him.
Virgil has seen Geri speaking and menacing
Dante with his finger, and Dante, who knows
why this soul is so angry and feels that he is
himself to some extent to blame,—if for no
other reason, because he is believed to be so by
the poor murdered soul,—becomes perturbed as
though from remorse and shame, and tender

for pity. Since he can do nothing more, he consecrates a small and most original family elegy to his relative, who cannot rest at peace owing to the cowardice and neglect of his own people. (One of the ancient glosses declares that Geri was finally avenged, thirty years after his death.)

We now enter what may be described as a city of pestilence. It is full of sick people and of corpses from which a putrid stench arises. Many images and comparisons confirm and reinforce the impression of disease and death, and the deviser of the infernal punishments obviously wishes to fix it in our minds. But the imagination is not overburdened by it; another impression follows, the grotesqueness of certain of these sick men, a grotesqueness that almost makes us smile. One of the damned is scratching himself furiously, so that Dante likens him to a groom, curry-combing a horse while his master waits, or wishing to finish quickly and get off to bed. He pulls crusts of scab off himself with his nails, as a fish is cleansed of its scales with a knife. Virgil almost congratulates him on his diligent activity and expresses the hope that he will continue to occupy himself thus agreeably forever.

Master Adam, shapeless from dropsy, becomes
" like a lute," his lips open from thirst, is not
able to get the rivulets of the Casentino, with
their cool and gentle flowing channels, out of his
mind. The poet, amused at the grotesque ex-
hibition and at all these extremes and contrasts,
makes Master Adam and the Greek Sinon quar-
rel. They have this in common, that they both
long for water and coolness; but their dispute
instead of relieving their common suffering,
seems rather to sharpen their respective egoism
and malignity. We find Dante in the act of
listening to them " quite fixedly," and then allowing himself to be reproved by Virgil, that is
to say, by himself. But though he reproves
himself, he has taken an interest more sympathetic than scornful in the strange amebæan
song, following this and that motive and feeling
its full plebeian force with admiration and satisfaction as one feels the skill and power of two
wrestlers. He has found something plebeian
within himself, however slight and fugitive,
without which he would never have listened or
looked on or become engrossed in the spectacle.
The reproof, the taking again possession of his
better self, is the superseding of this state, but it
is at the same time a recognition of that

plebeian element in himself; for what we have superseded we have lived. So broad and so sincere is the humanity of Dante.

The infernal journey hastens to its close amid monstrous sights and beings of colossal size. The giants are stationed like watch-towers; they represent the violence of brute strength now dominated and rendered impotent. We see Lucifer himself, that giant of giants, monster of monsters, with his three faces of three different colours, his three mouths, in each of which he champs a mighty sinner, his enormous woolly body and immense bat's wings. These are great natural curiosities, no less than the glacier in which bodies appear like straws in glass, and the poet describes them as if he had seen them, giving even the sense of effort and the impression of that arduous journey. Thus, for instance, he suddenly begins to feel " some wind " as he draws near to Lucifer's abode, and in the descent and ascent he clings to the wool of the King of the Inferno, and finally reaches the centre of the earth, and comes out by a small hole on the other side, and sees the stars. Certain intercalations vary this journey (which is like a journey to the pole), furious effusions of political and ethical hatred, in which Dante

presses yet further forward in the rhetorical
actio than he had gone in the cases of Filippo
Argenti and Pope Boniface. He takes Bocca
degli Abbati by the scruff of the neck in order to
compel him to name himself, and induces Friar
Alberigo to speak of himself by promising on
oath to remove the ice from his face; but he
does not keep this promise, because " to be
courteous " would in that case " be plebeian."
He makes these two tell him, in addition to the
account of their disgraceful lives, about the dis-
gracefulness of others, and thus hears of the
strangest prodigies, like that Branca d'Oria
who seems to be alive in the world " and eats
and drinks and sleeps and wears clothes," while
his soul is already in the glacier of the traitors
and a devil has taken his place in his body upon
earth. The speech is always Dantean, always
informed with poetry, but in these episodes
the violent Dante of whom we hear in the
biographies, has the upper hand of the poet,
and uses the powerful weapon of his poetry as
he was sometimes tempted to use the knife.

There is a notable page of pure Dantean
poetry in this part of the " Inferno," the episode of Ugolino: a bloody protest of injured
humanity against the vendetta and the punish-

ment that goes beyond the pale. Ugolino, whatever were his faults and crimes, is yet a man, and his executioners forget and tread under foot this quality in him; he now rises rightfully as judge of the judges, punisher of the punishers, executors of the executioners, and in this piling of horror upon horror, his crime disappears or fades into shadow and his reason shines out because, however ferociously and savagely, he nevertheless does avenge humanity. The old sinner and traitor suffers generously in prison among his innocent sons and nephews, condemned to die of hunger like him. He is tortured rather by the thought of their sufferings than his own. He is not staunch on his own account, but for those others, those innocent striplings, who either cry out for bread or are ready to die for their desperate father and would sacrifice themselves for him. Or they ask childishly for help, for that help which they are accustomed to ask but which he is no longer able to give. Revolt bursts out in the heart of Dante; in his invective against Pisa it grows into the image of the guilty city punished by the conglomeration of the islands and damming of the Arno so that all the inhabitants are drowned. It is an image which expresses the strength of his revolt in all its pitiless energy, and for this reason the passage has an intrinsically different sound, rhythm, and colour from the invective against the Genoese with which the episode of Branca d'Oria is concluded.

CHAPTER V

THE PURGATORIO

At the beginning of the " Purgatorio " we experience a sensation of relief at the same time sweet and comforting. It is as though we had come to the top of a steep ascent; we have left the sad places, desolate and gloomy, behind us, the tempest and the night of toil are past. Here is an island beaten upon by the sea; the reeds that surround it are bending to the waves; it is dawn. A soft hue of sapphire extends to the horizon and the star of Venus makes the whole east to smile. On the west four stars are shining, new to the eyes of the pilgrims, and the heavens seem to delight in their vivid rays. The charm of novelty appears to double the pleasure caused by their light. In these first heart-beats of the new poem we feel everywhere a dewy freshness. Soon after, the eye discovers in the remote distance " the trembling of the surface of the sea."

The silence is complete during the first mo-

ments and we meet with no one at all; but all
of a sudden there appears, one knows not
whence nor how, an old man, austere and decorous of aspect. This is the first meeting or the
first adventure of this part of the journey.
The old man is the guardian of Purgatory and
was once great Cato upon earth. The words
which he addresses to the two pilgrims become
an interrogatory, almost an anticipatory reproof. But one of the two has immediately
recognised him and weaves into his explanations
reverent allusions to Cato, to his past life, his
heroism and his domestic affections. " Flatteries," the old man calls them as he sets them
aside and proceeds to instruct the two pilgrims
in the rite which they must accomplish. Cato
is the character by which the poet gives actuality
to one of the sides of his ethical ideal. He is
rigid rectitude, the fulfilment of lofty duty,
which it seems cannot be achieved and cannot
act upon others so as to make them also realise
it, without a certain roughness, without the habit
of a certain degree of reticence and diffidence on
the part of one who is constantly watching himself and others. For this reason, Cato keeps
himself at a distance and answers only as much
as is strictly necessary; he does not converse,

but opens his mouth only to reprove and reject,
to direct and stimulate.

The pleasant sight of the newly discovered
land and the beautiful dawn along the sea-
shore, and the fresh grass, brings the life back
to the sad and weary countenance of the traveller out of Hell. Now he sees the bark of souls,
coming upon the waters and guided by an angel
with the sole movement of his star-pointing
wings. Something rapid and glistening white
(the whiteness of the wings) it seems, and of
increasing brilliance, a paradisiacal flashing
sign, coming and going quickly and leaving the
troubled souls behind upon the beach. It is the
first of such apparitions made of whiteness and
light; further on we shall see beautiful white-
clad creatures with faces " trembling like the
morning star with light," and those who lead
the two pilgrims upward " with wings open like
the wings of swans " fanning them as they go—
sensible forms of all that can be conceived most
pure spiritually, with no motive other than the
law divine of goodness and justice. Meanwhile the souls just now transported hither
from the earth are, like the two pilgrims, new
to the place, and questions and explanations are
asked and given between the equally inexperi-

enced travellers.   One thinks that Dante must
have much enjoyed travelling, both in reality
and imagination, the seeing of new places, knowing new people and things, the incidents, the unexpected encounters, half joyful and half astonished, the crossing of plains and the climbing of
mountains, the spring morning, the cheerful
sense of air and sun and grass and growing
plants.

He is recognised by his friend Casella, and
recognises him in turn and embraces him.   It is
Casella the artist, reminding him of his youthful
odes and of the pleasure he used to take in hearing them sung by his friend.   A new joy is now
added to his delight in nature after the horrors
of the infernal regions, a new happiness is called
into being at the names of poetry and music,
and with those names comes the desire to have
the things themselves and to feel their overt
power.   So Casella sings; he sings a celebrated
ode of Dante's own; and all present, both
Dante and Virgil and the souls who came along
with the singer, are enraptured at the notes " as
though the mind had no thought but them."
Who interrupts that song?   Who breaks into
that rapture?   It is the honest ancient, Cato,
who comes to join and to reprove them bitterly

for their slowness in proceeding towards the world of Purgation. The souls become fearful and flee towards the coast in disorder, like doves from fields where they have been feeding quietly; and Virgil and Dante also hasten, seized with shame. It is a scene of confusion and of trepidation, but all irradiated with a benign smile. Beautiful (it seems to say) it is, beyond doubt, to go to Paradise; but song, too, is beautiful and man so weak that among his other weaknesses this one of enjoying art, although it does distract him for a moment from urgent duty, is not the gravest; it is indeed " a little fault," a fault of youths, of men who deserve to be reproved here as youths and who, like youths, run away on the appearance of the severe pedagogue.

One of the usual misunderstandings about Dante's shadow gives an opportunity for certain words of Virgil's, of which it may be said that if the libretto is bad the music is good. It is the swift but soberly restrained effusion of one who has lived and worked, who knows difficulties and errors, has suffered and still suffers, and now warns others while he sighs for himself: " and here he bent his brow and said no more and remained troubled." Meanwhile we have arrived at the foot of a mountain so rugged and steep that it is impossible to ascend, and some other way must be found for safe climbing. Other souls are now met with on this shore in files or groups, and in them the poet expresses the gentle feelings of which he is now full: delicacy, shame, calm, resignation, peace, mansuetude, pardon for offences endured, universal benevolence. Certainly these souls once had other qualities and emotions far more keen, even violent and sanguinary; but now they are changed and grown gentle, they look back upon the past and smile, now they are outside that tumult in which they hardly know how they could once have taken so violent a part. The life of eternal salvation is no longer confused with the earthly life,—although they remember the offences from which they have suffered, the wounds they have received, the injustices of others and their own mistakes and sins. And Dante places in this gentle and serene spiritual condition one of those characters for whom (whether or not he realised these conditions in the contingencies of political life) he experienced great admiration and a sort of love, the love of the man who is moved by the valiant, the great, the noble, the artistic. This is Manfred, the chivalrous king of Sicily, hunted to death by the Popes, hated by the Guelphs, guilty of grave crimes, but " golden-haired and fair and of a noble mien," and gentle of heart, well worthy of finally turning to God and obtaining salvation.   The soul of man is not responsible before men, but only before Him " who willingly doth pardon."   He raises up the soul, while the churchmen wreak vengeance upon the body fallen in battle, and the unburied bones are beaten by rain and wind.   No polemical or partisan accent renders bitter what Manfred utters here; henceforth he judges pope, cardinals and himself indifferently, and sees where each was right or wrong.

The smile which illuminates the first cantos of the " Purgatorio " in various ways and with varying intensity, now condescending but contained, now bland and reconciled to men and things, almost dissolves in laughter at the beginning of the ascent of the Mount of Purgation. Supported by his guide, Dante climbs upward with effort and difficulty to the edge of the first circle.   He sits down and asks for an explanation of the new position of the sun, and, going back in thought to the ascent and its severity, enquires how much further they have still to go.

No sooner has Virgil given him the information
he seeks and comforted him with the picture of
the repose he will enjoy when he has arrived at
the goal, than a voice, half ironic and half
fatigued, is heard from behind a great rock.
The voice gives vent to the following reflection:
" Perchance thou wilt have need of rest before
that." It is one of his acquaintances of earth,
Belacqua, the supremely lazy one, who is here
in Purgatory just what he used to be upon earth
in his shop at Florence. Here he is, seated,
clasping his knees and holding his face between
his hands. For Belacqua, Dante who sets himself to solve astronomical problems, is mad or
extravagant, while he himself is wise and nor-
mal in his indifference to such useless researches.
Dante is wrong too in exhausting himself in
climbing, while he, Belacqua, is right in taking
things quietly. He explains the wisdom of his
attitude: " To hasten would be useless labour;
what is the advantage of climbing up?" Besides he would not have been able to enter Paradise in any case. But Dante is no Don Quixote,
lacking in the sense of reality, nor does Belacqua
express the good sense of a Sancho Panza. He
is rather the voice of laziness, which calls to
us in the midst of our exertions, but which has

no terrors for us, we know it so well. We do not even have to be on our guard when we meet him, and can crack jokes with him and recognise what little of reason he may possess in the midst of his exaggerations. "Take things without overmuch of keenness"; Belacqua is not altogether wrong, although the advice comes from a pulpit which inspires little faith or respect. On this account, Dante's lips are " a little disposed to laughter." In the last analysis we must laugh at ourselves, even when we seem to be laughing at others.

We are always hearing of deaths, assassinations, tortures and the like, taking place in mysterious circumstances in real life, leaving almost no trace behind; and these we carry with us in our hearts, full of sympathy and pity as well as curiosity. Three such cases are now recalled to us in the poem by the characters of Jacopo del Cassero, Buonconte, and Pia. The first of these had made an enemy of the lord of Este, who pursued him to the death, catching him precisely at the moment when he thought himself safe, as he was passing through Paduan territory. He fled and would have escaped and remained among the living had he taken another direction and avoided the marsh in which he was captured and killed. This life, which ended in a strenuous effort to escape its fate, and almost succeeded in doing so, has all our pity—this life extinguished in some solitary nook by the river's source. The second is the type of the valiant enemy, combated, feared and admired, but disappearing all at once in the heat of battle, perishing no one knows how, by an unknown hand in an obscure place, without leaving any trace. Imagination replies to eager curiosity with suppositions and possibilities. Buonconte, in flight and wounded to the death, invokes the name of Mary and is saved; but the demon, angered at seeing the angel bear off the soul, gives vent to his wrath on the insensible body, causing it to be carried away and lost in the swollen river, and the stiff arms, folded in death as a symbol of humble dedication of the mortal to divine justice and mercy, become uncrossed. Dante here lets himself go in the pleasure of supplying from memory and imagination the particulars of a certain historical day, the battle of Campaldino, when a storm followed the Florentine victory. Finally, the Pia was well known for her piety and kindness and hence it sufficed to call her " the Pia." Her words are so delicate that they seem to be rather sighed than said and they accompany as with music the utterance of that poor and gentle name. They are very feminine, and are well calculated to make us anxious for the distance still to be travelled, and for the repose of him to whom they are addressed (" and rested from thy long journey "). She recalls the place of her birth and the place where she perished, and refers without naming him to the man whom she must certainly have loved upon a time and who had married her and knows how and why she perished. He knows it, since he who gave her the wedding ring gave her also death.

These souls crowd about the pilgrim and beg that they may be prayed for on earth, for they know that he will return thither. He has such difficulty in freeing himself from their insistence that the passage becomes a bit altered in tone, and we smile a little when we meet with the comparison of the game of dice,—the bystanders abandoning the loser to crowd round the winner and the former thinking sadly of the chances, " going over the incidents of the game and acquiring sad experience." The bystanders attach themselves to the winner and dog his footsteps for gifts; he answers each one as he can and does his best to defend himself from the

annoyances attendant upon victory. The
ethico-political dialogue with Virgil on the
efficacy of prayer, absurd in the subtlety of its
theological solution, also brings us a feeling of
smiling happiness when Virgil utters the name
of Beatrice and Dante suddenly perceives that
the ascent is more easy and almost urges his
guide to hurry on.

But Dante seems now to have had his fill of
the soft and gentle figures he has been drawing
and turns himself again for a moment to his
true ideal, to the properly Dantean ideal of
energetic will and passion, free now from any
admixture of the infernal, and purified and complete in the dignity of virtue. Sordello stands
aside and alone, proud and disdainful, giving no
sign of astonishment and not uttering a word,
looking upon them " like a couchant lion."
The Farinata of Purgatory, he too, has his
great and silent love for his country, and at the
sound of the name of his birthplace he springs
to his feet, as moved and as affectionate now as
he was previously cold and unmoved. The
whole of Sordello is given in these few terzinas
and therefore he is unforgettable. When he
afterwards descends from his pedestal and
abandons his poetical attitude in order to ac-

company the travellers, he is but a quiet guide, giving them information and becoming with a change of style simply " the good Sordello."

Sordello is also of use to the poet in providing him with the text for two poetical outbursts: the invective against Italy and the judgment of the present princes as compared with their fathers. These passages are magnificent and powerful; the political judgment of the princes becomes transformed into a picture, where we see the sons behind their fathers, who occupy the foreground of the picture, and both are most solidly portrayed. We see Wenceslas behind Ottocar of Bohemia, who is trying to comfort his former rival Rudolph of Hapsburg, and lamenting some fault which causes him remorse. This Wenceslas is " bearded and delighting in ease and luxury." Philip, the Bold, " he of the small nose," takes council with Henry of Navarre, " so benign of aspect," and both are angry and distressed on account of their son and son-in-law, Philip the Fair, " the pest of France." The invective against Italy bursts out unexpectedly and is a true digression (as indeed the poet says); it is too long and elaborate to suit the situation, which is only capable of supporting the first three terzinas.

Dante gives vent to a complete piece of oratory, with divisions, transitions, exclamations, exhortations, ironies, sarcasms; although under the influence of passion, he forgets nothing which it is possible to say to further his political aim.

Poetry of the feelings reappears when Dante, declaring that it is vain to listen to political matters, turns away from Sordello and loses himself in the scene taking place around him. He is face to face with the mystery of prayer against temptation. There is a group of shades in the little valley, that " gentle army " which repeats its prayers and then gazes upward as though in expectation, " pale and humble." Fear and hope, confidence and the lack of it, sense of weakness before temptation and sense of security, meet together in the act. The soul becomes suffused with mingled pain and love at this hour of melancholy, when the sun has set and the evening is drawing in, the hour when travellers and navigators most feel the need of their home and of dear friends, and when the heart aches at the sound of a bell calling to complines.

The drama of conquered temptation becomes external, and therefore a little more superficial, during the combat that follows between the two angels who descend from heaven and drive away the evil serpent.   It is a kind of sacred representation of which there are other instances in the " Purgatorio."   In the pauses there are inserted some terzinas in which we are permitted to share in Dante's affection for a friend and for that friend's daughter who, unlike the wife who forgot him in another but less happy marriage, still remembers him.   There are also other terzinas, full of gratitude and praise for a lordly house which had received and protected the poet in exile.

At the gate of Purgatory, Dante does not climb over, but is transported by grace during a supernatural sleep.   He dreams, but his dream is not one of the usual allegories; it is rather the translation into terms of the imagination of what really happens to him.   He dreams that an eagle seizes him, as it seized Ganymede, and bears him upward to the sphere of fire, where the burning sensation of contact with the red-hot sphere into which he is entering, coincides with his awakening.   Then he resumes his journey, meeting new and wonderful things: the gate of Purgatory, the angel who mounts guard over it, the ceremonial with which it is opened.

to 'him. On the slope of the first level space he looks and sees carved a series of high reliefs, and further on a series of low reliefs set in squares, the former representing incidents of remarkable humility, the latter of pride tamed and punished. He describes the principal of these, but in such a way that the feeling aroused is rather one of admiration for the triumphal art than one of penitence and mortification. As we have previously admired the power of song as it flowed from the lips of Casella, so now we admire the power of sculpture, which here attains to perfection of self-expression by superhuman means or by the aid of genius, and to which is poured forth a hymn of praise. The first series of scenes, shining in the whiteness of marble, is speaking (we avail ourselves of the characteristics given by the poet), the second, mute but living, living still in the slaughter and death which it portrays. Dante seizes art at the moment when it enters the soul and no longer appears either sensuously or intellectually as the effect of this or that sense. It is a "visible speaking," something which at the same moment sees, touches, hears and smells, yet is none of those senses taken separately; reflection says "no" and "yes" concerning them, at the same instant. Such are, however, always the effects of the expression in the terms of one art of the representations of another art, proving that there are no fixed boundaries between them. One is embraced by the other, and sculpture would not be sculpture, were it not spoken by him who creates or re-creates it in speech, and poetry would not be poetry, were it not sculptured by him who creates or recreates it in sculpture. The angel of the Annunciation opens his mouth and says "*Ave!*" and the Virgin re-plies: "*Ecce Ancilla Dei;*" the imperial en-signs, though motionless, are still stirred by the wind; the little widow near Trajan's horse "in an attitude of tears and pain" still has her dialogue with the emperor,—a scene silent in the stone but living in the spirit, and repeated and relived by the poet.

The series of striking representations to be found throughout the "Purgatorio" begins with the meeting with the souls of the proud, bent double beneath heavy weights, the envious with their eyebrows stitched, the angry in the smoke, the slothful obliged to run, the avaricious face downward, the greedy languishing amid hunger and thirst, the lustful burning in fire. One might call these also low or high reliefs, finished to perfection with a single word, so clearly do they stand out. Here are the proud, like caryatids supporting a building with mighty effort; they pain the beholder. Next to them come the envious, clad in garments of a pale colour, leaning against a dull rock and thrusting out their chins as though short-sighted; then the greedy, all skin and bone—the eye-socket appears in their faces " like a ring without a gem." All these sufferers are portrayed as expiating their faults. They are conscious of guilt, and have a claim to virtue in their recognition of this and in the resignation with which they accept the new conditions in which they find themselves; for, though painful, they admit the justice of their fate and that it will result in good. The poet sympathises and respects the sufferers in his heart. He records their sins, but also portrays their gentleness and mildness and irradiating hope.

This is the general sentiment which penetrates the account. For the most part, and for his own reasons, Dante does not go beyond the particular story of this or that soul. But parallel and derivative feelings or emotions occur

as side issues.   In the first level stretch, among
the sinners for pride, we find Omberto Aldobrandesco still boasting that he is the son of a
" great Tuscan," no less an one than Guglielmo
Aldobrandesco, of ancient blood and celebrated
for the brilliant achievements of his ancestors.
From the lips of Oderisi of Gubbio flows the
lyric of the passing of human glory, something
between melancholy and resignation.   In Pro-
vanzan Salvani, we see pride conquering itself
all at once by a generous effort of the soul.
What can be more obvious than the confusion of
immortal glory with fame? Only here and there
has a philosopher disassociated the two conceptions and shown that the immortal glory is
in the work and its eternal efficacy, whether the
name with which it was first associated is remembered or not.   But he who does not disasso-
ciate the two (and to do so completely is
hard for the individual, desirous as he is
that something, his name at least, should
survive of his own individual life), is soon
overcome by the sentiment of the vanity
of effort, of the *omnia vanitas,* of pessimism and
defeat, which makes doing and not doing, living and dying,—dying as a child without ever
having done anything, or as an old man after

having done much,—alike indifferent; for everything is alike involved in forgetting. Such is the feeling which the poet reveals as he passes in review before his mind the yet recent names of those who have attained to fame in the art of painting or of poetry, throwing his own self into the whirlpool of future forgetting, although he is now rising in the sky of fame. And if this sentiment of vanity does not become desperate pessimism and cynicism in him, it is only because the image of the Eternal, which causes everything to melt away, is still for him the image of a divine Eternal in which duty and the joy of doing well find their existence, and which by overthrowing vainglory insures true glory. The proud Provenzano is at the summit of fortune which renders insolent even those who are not naturally so. But when he hears that his friend is a prisoner of war and awaiting ransom, he is so heart-broken that he throws pride to the winds and sets aside all shame. In the open square of Siena he begs charity of the passers-by in order to collect the ransom of his friend. Proud man as he is, there is something more than pride in him, something so energetic as to subdue his pride; he represents the triumph of human goodness over the most powerful obstacles, those within a man's own soul, a triumph all the more significant for that reason, and the more able to move the soul to rejoice.

Dante knows himself to be infected with the sin of pride, and confesses it with a good grace, speaking of his fear lest one day he be obliged to kneel down and be doubled up under the heavy weight of the expiatory stone. There is no profound repentance in this recognition; on the contrary, there is perhaps a shadow of satisfaction and fresh pride in the apparent humility. He confesses his pride in the very act of feeling himself free, so far as a man can be free, from the inelegant sin of envy. The little scene where he feels himself grown lighter (but does not know why) and, obedient to Virgil, feels his forehead and finds that one of the seven P's imprinted upon it by the angel is gone, has something graceful about it, made joyous by the almost boyish surprise, and fittingly brought to an end with Virgil's smile. The envious are not drawn with the sympathy bestowed on the portraits of the proudly great. These are selected artists like Oderisi, or generous spirits like Provenzano. Envy, on the contrary, is drawn as a singular and incomprehensible disease, a monstrosity, a folly. This appears in

the narrative of the Sienese lady who tells of
the incomprehensible fire in her blood, and of
her strange attitude of soul, owing to which she
enjoyed the injury of others far more than her
own good fortune; suffered when she saw a
happy man; was without pity for her fellow
citizens; and prayed God that He would allow
these to be beaten in the war they were about
to undertake against the Florentines. She rejoiced in their having to take to flight, and in
the pursuit of them by their enemies, and felt
when things were in that state that she had
attained to the summit of good fortune and
happiness.

And now Dante is again seized with the rage
for politics. The shape of a ridge of Purgatory
recalls to him a part of Florence, that well-
governed city, as he sarcastically describes it,
and the sight of the envious lady of Siena suggests to him a satire on the Sienese ("vainer
than the French"). He amuses himself with
their megalomania and illusions, with the water
of the Diana and with the port of Talamone
which has swallowed up so much labour and
money. They already believe that they see the
fleets ready to weigh anchor, which they never
will do, and parade about as admirals, which

they never will be.   In the mouth of Guido del
Duca he places an account of the various peoples who dwell on the banks of the Arno.   They
are represented as swine, curs, wolves and foxes.
The same character talks of the decadence and
corruption of the inhabitants of the Romagna,
sighing in vain for bygone times and for the
race which is no more, a race of virtuous women
and knights well skilled in noble diversions and
exercises, all alike animated with love and courtesy.   Here folk dream and lament, weep and
are full of scorn; politics become soul-absorb-
ing.   Further on, Marco Lombardo draws a
similar portrait of Lombardy, where the old
tradition holds its own against the new only
in the persons of three old men; Hugo Capet
vehemently denounces his degenerate and per-
verse descendants and takes consolation in the
vengeance God is preparing in secret; Forese
bursts out in invective of the shameless Florentine women,—but here we are sensible of personal feeling, for the outburst is not quite in
place and the tone is rhetorical.

In this part of the " Purgatorio," ecstatic or
dream visions are numerous.   We surprise the
poet in the act of abandoning himself to them
or of waking up from them, his mind turned

back upon itself, closed to all penetration from
without. He is astonished at this power of the
imagination, which steals a man from the surrounding world and which cannot come from
anywhere but heaven; and so absorbed is he in
the images that carry him away, that he moves
forward with eyes veiled and limbs out of control, " like a man affected with wine or sleep."
Then, all of a sudden, his soul returns to the
things " which are outside it and are true." Or
he wanders from thought to thought confusedly
and talks wildly, mingling one thing with another, until the eyes close and thought becomes
transmuted into dream. What are the phan-
tasms in which the mind thus loses itself? They
are traces of things heard or read and are called
into memory by their connection with the emotional life of the moment. This in turn becomes
intensified by them, with vivid strokes and gestures and words which cut into the soul. A
memory of Jesus leaving His parents and going
to dispute with the doctors, becomes condensed
into the vision of the temple full of people and
of a woman entering and saying in the soft,
sweet tones of a mother: " My son, wherefore
hast thou done this to us? " The story of
Pisistratus is given in its closing scene, that

of the dialogue between Pisistratus and his wife, which contains the benign philosophical reply of the king.   The life of Saint Stephen is concentrated in the moment when the youth sinks to earth beneath the blows of his assassins, raising his eyes to heaven and praying God that he may pardon his persecutors.   Out of the last book of the "Æneid" is drawn a young girl who weeps bitterly and says: "O queen, wherefore hast thou wished to take thy life in anger?" Less happy, that is to say, somewhat artificial, is the vision of the stammering woman, which occurs a little further on; it is an image-concept, altogether neither image nor concept, and has in it something of the allegorical in a depreciatory sense.

Here, too, the didactic interludes begin to become frequent and extended.   Virgil makes clear how it happens that the more the love of God is distributed the more it enriches its possessors.   Marco Lombardo refutes the false notion that the corruption of the world is due to the influence of heaven, showing its origin in the mind of man, who has simply not known how to maintain the distinction between the two powers that must rule society, the sword and the pastoral staff.   Virgil, again, explains a page of the ethics of good and evil as due to incorrect, false, excessive or defective love, and shows what the natural inclination of love is, and how moral liberty enters into it. Statius discourses of physics and physiology, developing the theory of generation. In this doctrinal poetry Dante does not represent the laborious self-creation of the truth, or the enthusiastic spirit knowing itself to be the announcer of original and revolutionary truths, nor is he concerned with the shock of opinions and arguments in dialogue and polemic. He presents solely the relation between pupil and master; the learner goes to the school of the possessors of that knowledge which he lacks and attends to their teaching. At the conclusion of one of his explanations, Virgil looks attentively in Dante's face to see if he is satisfied, and Dante is already eager to put further questions, but remains silent, owing to timidity. Virgil, however, perceives that " the timid will fails to make itself clear " and encourages him to be bold. Dante is afflicted with a like timidity in the presence of Statius; he is tempted to ask questions, stays himself, then tries again, like (as he says) " to the young stork, which opens its wings, wishing to fly, but does not leave the

nest." Virgil encourages him and says smil-
ingly: "Loose the bow of speech, which thou
hast drawn up to the arrow's head." All
through this poetry we find the attitude of the
teacher knowing his own thought, wishing to
make it clear, and inclining towards the pupil
to embrace him and raise him up to the truth.
Consequently, the thoughts expressed assume
the brightness of bodily forms. Substantial
form, at once distinct from and united to matter, possesses a specific virtue which we feel only
when it is in action; it reveals itself only in its
effect " like the life of the plant by its green
leaves." The first notions and the first appe-
tites are present in man " like the desire of the
bee to make honey." God intervenes when the
articulation of the brain is reached in the process of the formation of the fœtus: " The First
Mover turns towards him glad to see such art
in nature "; he seems to admire what nature,
created by him, has created, and breathes into
it the possibility of intellect " and makes one
soul of it, which lives and feels and depends
upon itself,"—as in another comparison the
heat of the sun linking itself to the sap which
flows from the vine, transforms itself into wine.
But it would be to diminish the poetry of Dante

to confine it to these splendid sensible images
with which it is everywhere flowered. It is poetical in its own movement, which imprints itself
with imaginative clarity upon the details, whatever they may be, of the dilemmas and syllo-
gisms. Here we find dialectic converted into
an enjoyable æsthetic spectacle; and here truly
the philosophy " falls in love with itself," to
quote one of the didactic odes.

Characters of the human drama continue to
appear among these visions and during the
exposition of these doctrines. Pope Adrian V is
found face downward among those who are
expiating the sin of avarice. He had been pope,
but now is simply one soul among others, naked
like them, and he tells Dante, who kneels down
before him as though he were still invested with
the supreme dignity, that he is now as others
are, simply " a fellow servant " of the same
power, God. Greedy and ambitious, he had
risen as high as the papacy, but the month or little more during which he held the supreme office, did not satisfy his ambition; it made him, on
the contrary, feel its emptiness, revealed to him
the falsity of human existence, and inspired him
with the sense of responsibility and humility.
Risen so high, he became aware of his own

smallness and misery. Nor is he now able to comfort himself with the thought of the devotion of his friends and relations, clients and courtiers, all of them wicked and selfish. When he thinks of the earth, he can only discover one among the crowd of those still living, a niece named Alagia, who would be good, in spite of the bad example of her relatives, and he sends to her his affectionate greeting and silently hopes for her prayers: "For she alone is left to me there below."

Who has not sometimes wished to conquer death and see again the dear ones he has lost, to resume affectionate discourse with them about familiar and beloved things, to learn of them things previously unknown and to tell them what has occurred since the last meeting, just as though one were seeing them for the first time after a long voyage? Feelings of this kind inspire Dante's poetical meeting with Forese Donati, the friend of his youth, the companion of his pleasures and mistakes. He disputed and got angry with him, but yet loved him, weeping bitterly when death carried him away. How full and splendid was their life together! "What thou wast with me and I with thee!" Now they are silent about their common follies, or only refer to them in a veiled manner; but the pure part of their common memories is recalled, together with the dear ones connected with those sweet moments: the good wife of Forese, whom he calls "my Nella," my "little widow," who has not forgotten him, but has preserved her faith in him and has wept and prayed for him; and the sister Piccarda, "my sister, of whom I know not whether she were more beautiful than good or more good than beautiful" . . . and who is now awaiting him in Paradise. The friendship thus purified revives, sweet and tender, and since they have walked some distance together and Forese has shown him some of the things and people of the place in which they now find themselves, and they must again separate provisionally, his friend asks him lovingly and longingly, as though he had forgotten the earth and death, and as though the separation were for a new journey: "When shall I see thee again?" The other incidents appertaining to this episode, such as the invective against the women of Florence, which we have already mentioned, or the prediction of the approaching murder of Corso

Donati, are not connected with the poetical meaning; they are there because Dante wished them to stand there for his own purposes.

Who has not been present at the meeting of two men who have loved and esteemed one another by hearsay and witnessed their emotion when an accident finally brings them together unexpectedly and the one speaks of his desire to know the other, and they stand thus revealed to one another and smiles are mingled with their emotion and astonishment? This is the poetic motive of the meeting between Statius and Virgil. Dante may perhaps have thus imagined himself meeting the great ones of the past, when he had made himself worthy of them and like them had been carried on the wings of fame. He may have dreamed of meeting them as their disciple but as a disciple who has done honour to his masters and surpassed them, while they in turn recognise with pleasure and admiration the dependence of the pupil, his new thoughts and discoveries, his new and beautiful works which in some measure are their own, since they are born of their labours. " I would remain another year in Purgatory to see Virgil," says Statius, who does not know he is in his presence. And Virgil smiles and turns to

Dante " with a look that silently says: be
silent "; and Dante in his turn smiles and nods
to Virgil, and makes him known to the other.
A conversation begins between the two Roman
poets, and Statius who has made progress and
become a Christian, although secretly, is able
to say that not only through Virgil, through the
"Æneid," did he become a poet, since it was his
spiritual mother, his nurse, and his perpetual
rule of art, but that from Virgil, from his
prophetic poetry, he received the impulse toward the new faith, the lot of blessedness:
" Thou didst as those who walk by night and
bear a light behind them, which helps them not
but shows the way to those that follow." And
then he asks for news of their colleagues in
poetry and literature, " Terence our senior,"
of Cecilius, Plautus and Varro; and Virgil gives
him this news and news of others, and of that
Greek, " whom the Muses suckled more than
ever they did another," and of the heroes and
heroines whom Statius had sung in his poems.
The heart of Dante swells with love and desire
when he hears speech of such things, and hears
praise of the poet and of poetry, " the name
which most endures and bestows most honour."
He listens enraptured to the names of the great

poets and of the legendary heroes, about whom
the two converse as of persons well known to
them.   Their discourse introduces him to the
secrets of poetry.   The whole scene is very rich
in detail by comparison with the summary treatment and mere list of names with which the
same motive is treated at the beginning of the
" Inferno."

In the succeeding cantos the attention shifts
from ancient literature to modern and contemporary.   Professions of faith, judgments
favourable and otherwise, and polemical criticism take the place of solemn admiration and
praise of poetry in the abstract.   Dante enun-
ciates the theory to which he holds in his love
poetry; he salutes the " father of me and of
others, my betters," in Guido Guinicelli, who
once composed sweet and graceful love-poetry;
he asserts the superiority of Arnaldo Daniello
over all other poets and writers of romances;
he notes the loss of reputation of rhymers in the
vulgar tongue, finding in that result a confirmation of his own judgment about them and a
justification of his own course.   These verses
have all become celebrated in the history of
literature and have been constantly quoted, and
their critical importance is heightened by the

epigraphical and epigrammatic beauty of their form.

Dante seems to have been of opinion that poets, when they sin, do not do so through mean or base promptings, or through malignity, but only owing to incontinence and sensuality: Statius was among the spendthrifts, Bonagiunta among the greedy, Guido and Arnaldo are among the sensual. And Dante, too, must expiate his amorous sins, great or small, and pass through the flames; he seems to blush for shame, but it is a blush rather for the punishment than for the sin itself and for repentance of it. His does not seem to be real shame or distress, or humiliation, but rather the blush of a child detected in wrong-doing who perhaps knows that he will again be caught doing the same thing and will again blush for shame. His reluctant submission to the passage through the flames is represented as though he were a child being urged to endurance and reassured and comforted by being shown a beautiful apple which he will receive if he is good, the apple being nothing less, in this case, than the eventual sight of his beloved lady. Malice, irony? These are words that one never dares to utter about Dante, and certainly if they were uttered

in a marked manner they would be out of place;
but it is equally certain that the purity of his
affections, the spontaneity of his actions, and
his veracity as a poet, rebel at following set
paths and give form and shape to the most un-
looked-for situations, to strong as well as to
the most delicate shades of feeling. Alterna-
tion of the serious and the jocose is certainly
not impossible to him.

In all this wealth of scenes and discourse, the
gentle breath of sentiment which seems to blow
through the early cantos of the " Purgatorio,"
the sentiment of travel, of excursion, delightful
though it include the climbing of a steep mountain, is lost. Or, if it is not wholly lost, it is
felt only here and there, in such expressions, for
instance, as the poet uses when we find ourselves
before a deserted path in the mountain (" the
dull hue of the rock "), or when we are touched
by the " shining rays of the setting sun," and
obliged to shade our faces with our hands, or
when we again see the sun after having passed
through the wall of smoke, the sun weakly shining through the dense wet mist, or finally when
we contemplate the rather thin moon " made
like a burning cask." But that sentiment returns in all its fulness when we reach the top

of the mountain, where was once the earthly
Paradise. The evening is coming on, and
Virgil, Statius and Dante stop at a certain point
and stretch themselves out on the slope, resting
like a flock watched over by the shepherd. Beyond the overhanging rocks there is only a little
of the sky to be seen, but in that little there are
the stars, larger and more bright than usual.
Dante, waking with the rising of the sun, enters
eagerly "the divine forest dense and flour-
ishing."

What is this pleasant wood, in which there
appears to the poet a young woman singing
alone by herself and culling a flower from
amid the flowers? A good many critics have
been shocked at the profane colouring of
the picture and at the comparisons with
Proserpine and Venus, as not only out of
harmony with the general tone of Dante's
work, but with that situation in particular.
But we really do not understand why they
have waited for this point to feel scandal-
ised, for there are many parts of the cantos
we have already read which would have afforded an excellent opportunity for such criticism, if, contrary to our own practice, something
is sought in the "Comedy" which is not there,

and what is there is denied. For our part, we accept the twenty terzinas upon Matelda as one of the most beautiful of the many expressions of the 'longing which leads man to create enchanting landscapes animated with enchanting feminine figures. A large number of such gardens and little woods and little meadows and shepherdesses and fair young girls culling flowers and dancing and singing had lately appeared in Provençal and Italian poetry; and Dante again takes in hand the common motive with great delight, developing it to a new form of exquisite perfection, in which the fascination of youth, of beauty, of love and laughter, is exalted in every image: "Of lifting her eyes, she granted me the boon," "Erect upon the other bank she smiled," "Bearing full many colours in her hands . . .," "Singing like an enamoured lady. . . ." These images are all there is to Matelda, because in the second part of the canto she is used simply to perform the duty of giving information, though the "corollary" which she finally gives as a "grace" sounds, indeed, like a coquettish correction, and at the same time a confirmation of the ancient notions about the age of gold in which both Virgil and Statius believed. At any

rate, they smile when they hear her explanation,
and then she is called to other grave duties,
more or less allegorical, which have nothing to
do with the inspiration of which she, as a character in the " Comedy," was originally born. It
may be said that Dante had other and greater
inspirations than this; but what matters is that
he did have this one, and that it is beautiful
with its own particular beauty and grace. Even
the trace of artificiality of which we are sensible in the representation of the idyllic scene,
and still more in that of the lady, beautiful in
her every act, step and gesture, is perfectly in
its place in this picture. The effect attained is
a concrete representation of an abstract pleasure, the enjoyment at once of beautiful natural
scenery and of feminine beauty, two pleasures
which increase one another and melt into a
single impression of earthly beatitude.

As the poet walks side by side with Matelda,
he hears a melody and sees a fire lit afar in the
forest, and then the melody becomes distinct as
a song and the fire is better seen as due to seven
burning candlesticks, behind which are approaching twenty elders singing, two by two.
When these have passed, four animals advance,
each with six wings all full of eyes, and among

them a chariot drawn by a griffin, golden and
vermilion-white. Three women are dancing on
the right hand, one of them in garb of a ruddy
colour, the next of emerald, and the third snow-
white, and on the left are four clothed in purple,
dancing to the measure of one who has three
eyes in her forehead. Two old men follow this
procession, one in the dress of a doctor, the
other with a sword in his hand, and then four
others of humble aspect, and finally one who
walks in his sleep. When the procession has
stopped, a woman veiled in white appears on the
car, crowned with olive and dressed in a green
mantle over a garment the colour of flame. She
is Beatrice, who speaks to Dante, reproves him
and induces him to confess his faults and to
repent. She makes him plunge into Lethe, the
river of forgetfulness, and then at last casts
off her veil. The procession goes away again,
Beatrice descends from the car, and the griffin
ties it to the foot of a leafless shrub, which
thereupon recovers all its flowers and foliage.
Beneath the mystic tree Beatrice sits down surrounded by her ladies. In an instant an eagle
swoops down from heaven, rending the tree—
bark, leaf, and blossom—and striking the car.
A fox jumps into the car, but Beatrice drives it

away. The eagle then again descends, and leaves the car covered with its plumes, after which a dragon bursts out of the earth and breaks the car in pieces, carrying away a portion. The remaining parts of the car are then covered with plumes and put forth three heads with two horns, and four heads with one horn. The car becomes a monster, and on the monster is seated a harlot, whom a giant kisses and watches over; and when she looks around with ready eyes and fixes them on the poet, her lover scourges her from head to foot, and looses the monster and drags it through the wood. Then Beatrice announces to Dante the coming of a messenger of God, who shall slay the impious harlot and the equally impious giant who sins with her.

This scene from the last two cantos of the " Purgatorio " has been compared with a liturgical drama or an *auto sacramental;* and the comparison has some truth in it. But the strange and wonderful figures, acts and events, perform a function in striking the imagination and serving to fix the attention. They predispose the mind to receive a teaching or a warning, and this is then given in the story of the characters, or by the speeches placed in their mouths, or by a species of guide-book explanation. The images are without direct value as poetry, but they are the means for representing something else, just as to-day (without referring to traces of sacred dramas in the various festivals still celebrated in the remoter parts of the country) we employ illustrated alphabets for children, where a showy figure is to be seen beside each letter to attract the curiosity and fix the letter clearly upon the childish memory. When the illustration is wanting, when there is no explanation with the figures, what we see is simply a masquerade or sequence of strange images, wholly, or almost wholly, without coherence, and without any meaning external or internal. In the present case, the explanation is wanting, that is to say, the comments of Dante himself, and although it is possible to indicate the thought behind the whole thing, as more or less of a sequence (the history of the Church) and also to understand certain of its details clearly (the harlot and the giant, who signify the Church of Rome and the King of France), it is impossible to be sure of the meaning everywhere (the griffin shines " now with the one, now with the other nature," when the eyes of Beatrice are fixed upon it. Does that mean that theology,

devoted to Jesus, looks upon him now as God,
now as man?—or does it mean something else?)
Thus it would seem that we must conclude, as
indeed some critics do conclude, that what
Dante offers us is something between an unpoetical allegory and an unpoetical masquerade. But
if there be some truth in the comparison with
the liturgical dramas and the *autos sacramental,*
it is not all of the truth, nor yet wholly true.
The poet does not here compose such a drama,
with which he was familiar and in which he had
taken part, but (and the difference is essential)
remakes and imitates its effects.

In other words, the liturgical drama is here
reduced to the level of material; and whether
it be obscure or not as to its hidden meaning,
or partly obscure and partly clear, what pre-
dominates is the feeling of the poet, who sees
pass before his eyes one of the many images,
big with mysterious significance, to which biblical and Christian literature and sacred art had
accustomed men's minds. Hence the peculiar
poetry, which we feel and enjoy in spite of
everything, in this part of the poem is free from
the frigidity of allegory, because it does not
serve allegory, but presupposes and makes use
of it as material. A painting which does not

have its motive in itself, but in certain thoughts of which it is the conventional sign, is allegorical and unpoetical; but another painting, which might use the former as its material and which portrays the impression which it has aroused in the mind of the artist, may be neither unpoetical nor allegorical. Dante here expressly states his sources and his authors: " Read Ezekiel; John is with me." He admires with the eye of an artist the appearances which pass before him: " Not Rome delighted the African or even Augustus with so beautiful a car; that of the sun would be poor by comparison with it "; and he surrounds them with colours and sounds: " And behold a brightness ran suddenly from all parts through the great forest . . . and a sweet melody pervaded the luminous air. . . ."

The human drama is developed upon this system of decoration, apocalyptic in origin and construction as the commentators all believe; that is to say, in the midst of this poetry we find another, to understand which we must discount all allegorical meaning and forget what Beatrice is allegorically. Thus, too, the poet all of a sudden misses Virgil from his side, not human Reason or anything of that sort, but just Virgil, whom he and we have had as com-

panion and guide on the journey, and whose
figure is connected with all the impressions and
emotions which we have experienced. We feel
a pang when we become aware that he has dis-
appeared, that we have lost him. Again, Beatrice is simply the lady whom the poet loved in
his first youth, the ideal from which all other
ideals have derived their worth: generosity,
purity of life, happiness, affection, goodness,
noble toil, sublime religion. But she has been
separated from us; fortune, or death, or our
own fault, has removed her and our life has
pursued other ideals, narrow, inferior, change-
able, one following the other. We have been
driven towards them by impulses which have
gradually developed and asserted themselves
powerfully; or they have been due to accidents,
to the society in which we have found ourselves, to incidents in our careers, to the logic
of the passions, which has dragged us with it
in its course. But behold, when satiety and
nausea and remorse have laid hold upon us,
when we have felt ourselves poisoned with the
poison which our own feverish activity and passion have produced, when we are as far as possible distant and strayed from our path, she
again appears before us. We are changed and

weary, but she remains unchanged and indeed
has become more beautiful, vivid and radiant,
as the result of all that time and distance now
placed forevermore between ourselves and her.
We recognise her and bow our heads in a recognition which is something between pain and
shame. She recognises and reproves us, takes
compassion upon us and prepares to comfort
and sustain us because of the ancient ties which
still remain, because she was ours and shows herself to be ours still in the anguish, shame, and
perplexity in which we find ourselves immersed
and groping.

For the situation has become altogether different; Beatrice is here neither an allegory, nor
the Beatrice of the youthful poems and of the
youthful book of devotion. She is a character
bearing within itself the history of the former
Beatrice; and the past and the persistence of
her name confer upon her an aureole of memories. She is solemn, severe, wise and fully
aware, yet loving. Dante cannot love her as
he once loved. There is certainly love in the
hearts of both, but it is a love which henceforth
has a new intonation; Dante appears like a subject before her whom he loved in youth, become
a queen. He now hardly dares to love, and feels

to the full his lesser worth. Beatrice has before
her a lover and at the same time a son, weak
and gone astray. She loves him and is at the
same time maternal; maternal in the care she
takes of him, maternal when she frowns upon
him. All the dreams of youth return with her,
but more beautiful than they were before. They
return at that shining, majestic apparition,
veiled, yet recognised through the white veil.

The meeting between the two begins on a
note of reproof (a reproof conveyed by her
very presence, before she speaks). Then some
one's compassionate speech causes her frown to
relax, and melts her suffering heart and allows
the tears to flow. These bring their blessed relief and her whole being abandons itself to their
sweetness. The second moment brings remembrance. It is more calm; hopes and promises,
pleasant experiences of former days, and by
contrast, the straying from the way, which yet
could not alter love, pass in review. The third
moment is one of timidity and stammering, as
of one who cannot bear to fix his mind upon
the awful crudity of his sin. Then the meeting closes with a pang of remorse, so acute that
the man Dante faints, shaken by emotions, and
is plunged by the friend of Beatrice into the

pure waves of the river of forgetfulness. A little later, after he has beheld the mystery of the car and has heard the prophecy from Beatrice, and received his own mission from her, he again begins to discourse of his estrangement from her. He does not remember any evil or error of which he has ever been guilty, and says so candidly. Then Beatrice is able to smile upon him at last, to look benignly upon him and to reply:—" If thou dost not remember, at least thou wilt remember that thou hast drunk of the water of Lethe!"

VI

THE PARADISO

Figures and scenes, affectionate, tender, melancholy, graceful, such as we have been describing, gradually grow tenuous and finally lose themselves in the third poem, the third and last great collection of the lyrics of Dante's maturity. Henceforth Beatrice fulfils Virgil's task and becomes guide, teacher and interpreter. Having regained her, Dante immediately loses her in so far as she was the expression of his heart's ideal. The drama of love is silenced during the accomplishment of the great task of mounting with her from star to star, beholding, hearing, understanding all things. But it is not silenced completely, and a spark of affection shines here and there. Whilst she is pointing out and instructing, Beatrice is listened to as though she were an elder sister who has completed her course of studies and graduated with honour, teaching her younger brother who is still backward and uncertain in his learning, dis-

quieted and tortured by doubts, prejudices and
false conceptions. He often makes gross mistakes which she answers by treating him as if
he were a delirious child, now bearing with him,
now smiling at his " childish prattle " and foolish judgments, and undertaking patiently to
teach him. She is most beautiful, radiantly
lovely; she is the sweet guide " who smiles and
glows in the sight of the blessed," ever turning
" her face toward heaven." It is joy and rav-
ishment to behold her. She is aware of the fact
and like any woman is pleased at it. " Conquering me with the light of a smile, she turned to
me saying: ' Turn from me and listen, for not
in my eyes only does Paradise lie.' " At another
time when she assists at divine mysteries and
beholds manifestations of divine wrath, she is
again like a woman of flesh and blood, full of
nervous trepidation. When the sky reddens
during St. Peter's invective her face changes,
she becomes pale, " as a modest woman remains
unmoved on her own account, but is filled with
timid apprehension as she listens to the shame-
ful tale of another." At the conclusion she
leaves Dante's side and flies swiftly back to her
place among the blessed, where he sees her
girded with the light of God, " a crown reflect-

ing from itself eternal beams." From afar she looks at him and smiles, then immerses herself in God: " then she turned to the eternal fount." Here the mystical idea of love which in the lyric poetry of the new style had been expressed only superficially and in the abstract is developed poetically. Sensual love rises to intellectual love, earthly love to celestial, the one being simply the precursor of the other and finally merging and dying away in the other after one last flicker of life.

The opening of the poem introduces us to several figures which really belong to the family of those in the " Purgatorio." There is Piccarda, sister of Forese, for whom Dante had felt a fraternal regard as a good but fragile creature torn and trampled upon amongst the political passions of the age. She was a member of the Clarist sisterhood, haled from her convent and forced into marriage, but since at heart she remained the spouse of Christ, she appears here as a nun. She is a meek little creature among her sister-spirits, faintly distinguishable in the crystalline and lucid sphere, scarce outlined, evanescent, like a " pearl on a white forehead." Her words are happy, almost cheerful, pronounced " with smiling eyes " with

the joy of a pure soul in Paradise at seeing
once more her former friend. " My greater
beauty will not prevent your recognising me
. . . see . . . I am Piccarda." She replies
readily and affably to any just and reasonable
questions. Like Beatrice, though in a somewhat different manner, she smiles with amiable
condescension before answering the questions
put by Dante, the ignorant newcomer: " With
the other shades, she smiled a little." The convent from which she was snatched is for her
" the sweet cloister." Indicating one of her
companions, she points to the monastic wimple
covering her head as " the shadow of the sacred
bands." She speaks softly of the sacrilegious
act committed against her. The men involved
in it were not scoundrels, but rather " men more
accustomed to bad than to good." Her distracted existence as nun-wife is described in one
sigh of anguish as she thinks of the past. " God
knows what my life was then ! " The nun, accustomed to renunciation and to the joys of
obedience, here takes the same attitude in the
face of the judgment of God as in the former
world:—" Brother, the virtue of charity calms
our will, making us content with what we have,
thirsting for nought else."

To the same order of souls, but more rapidly delineated, belongs Romeo, whose honesty was called in question, but established by his austere renunciation, shining the brighter for his drab existence as a wretched old beggar. Further on there is Charles Martel, the young prince whom Dante loved and in whom he saw strong promise for the future, who speaks of the tragedy in the loss of a magnificent and beneficent royalty before it has been attained. With the introduction of Cunizza one gathers how much the third poem contains of human lyric quality, so abundant in the two former poems, human, that is to say, in the commonly accepted meaning of the term. Cunizza, though she was the great lover, the sinner in love, the *magna meretrix* of chroniclers, was so large-hearted and generous that no one could judge her severely, nor did she so judge herself, alleging that she was contented with her destiny and being so far from merely submitting to divine judgment that one might almost say she was willing to begin afresh in order to merit her portion of justice. At the end of the " Paradiso " is the figure of an old man, St. Bernard, a kind of calm and benevolent Cato, whose looks carry consolation with them: " In his eyes, on his cheeks, was the benignant

cheerful piety becoming to a loving father."
So full of cheerfulness and benignity is he that
these are the only means he employs to direct
Dante's eyes towards the splendour of God's
light: " Bernard accosted me, smiling, thus en-
gaging me to look on high." We have all of us
in our youth met dear old men like him, who
have in their own way shown us many high
and beautiful things to fill us with wonder and
joy.

The journey continues, becoming miraculous
in a manner only occasionally employed in the
preceding poems. The poet tells how he as-
cended without knowing it to the sphere of fire,
by gazing at the eyes of Beatrice, who kept hers
fixed on things eternal, a marvel which is repeated time after time in the ascent from sphere
to sphere. He rises really, soul and body,
drawn by a power which makes him light and
rapid as the lightning. He does not perceive
any movement, but is aware only of change in
his surroundings, made known to him by the
increase of beauty in the face of his guide. At
first, in the circle of the Moon, he has a sensation of penetrating a cloud " shining, thick and
solid " like a diamond flashing in the sun, and
of being incorporated in it in the way in which a

ray of light is received into water, without cutting it. Then he passes to light even more
vivid, to lakes of light which reflect lights still
more intense, lights from the radiance of which
arises marvellous song; sanctity of soul and
divine goodness and majesty unite in producing
an inebriate giddiness both of sense and spirit.
The tone of the narrative becomes admiring, ex-
clamatory, enthusiastic, ecstatic. " That which I
saw seemed to me to be the laughter of the
universe, for its inebriation entered into me
through hearing and sight. O joy! O ineffable
pleasure! O essential life of love and peace!
O certain wealth without desire! " This tone
dominates the last poem, sustaining and in-
volving all other tones.

Still, in the midst of this overflow and perpetual increase of light, amongst these inebria-
tions, the poet does not abandon his attitude
as of an inquisitive and attentive traveller, ob-
serving and describing as he goes. His sight, as
he says in one place, does not " fail him," but
" takes in the why and wherefore of all this
happiness "; he examines everything minutely,
remembering he will have to write about it
later, like a pilgrim•beholding the temple of his
vows who " hopes to describe it as it appears."

Thus he gives a detailed account of the marvellous and amazing effects of light which he is allowed to contemplate, having recourse in order that all may be clear and plain, to familiar figures out of everyday life. A triple circle of " many lightnings " bright and gleaming and resounding with song, which disposes itself around him, is represented by a troop of girls dancing and singing as they dance, who stop, not because the dance is finished, but " silently listening " to catch the refrain upon the lips of the leader and repeat it as they resume the dance. When these lightnings have ended their song, each settles itself in its original place " like candle in candlestick."   From the two arms of a luminous cross, and from top to base, lights run and flash brilliantly as they meet at the intersection; just as in a ray of sunshine from half-closed shutters we see minute particles of dust darting hither and thither, slowly or swiftly, perpetually shifting and changing their position.   Another array of lights disposes itself in the form of a luminous eagle, making the many voices of the souls to issue forth as one. The murmur of sound swells into a distinct voice, rising through the neck of this singular bird " as through a round pierced hole," and is

compared with the sound formed in the neck of
the cithern, and the breath which is forced into
a reed-pipe through the apertures. Two of the
lights of the souls which compose the eyebrow
of the eagle are specially mentioned in the
course of its speech, and they flicker tremu-
lously as they listen to the words, just as a good
lute-player when accompanying a good singer
follows the voice with vibration of the strings.
Indeed the comparison is strengthened by the
simile: " the concord is as complete as when
eyelids blink together." Again, other lights
dispose themselves in concentric spheres which
appear to the observer to dance on " fixed
poles," flaming strongly " like comets," and
more or less rapidly in accord with the intensity
of their beatitude. The poet compares them
with the mechanism of clockwork, in which the
wheels go round in such a way that to the looker-
on the principal movement seems " quiet and
the last to move." The angelic hosts ascend
and descend to and from the rows of saints
like swarms of bees which sip the blossoms and
return to the hive to distil their honey before
returning anew to the flowers. Sometimes the
laborious process by which he seeks to describe
celestial spectacles vividly is abbreviated. Imag-

ine, says the poet, " you who desire to understand," imagine fifteen stars of the greater
magnitude in addition to the seven stars of Ursa
Major and two of the Minor arranged in two
ensigns in the sky, twelve stars each, turning in
two circles one behind the other, " and you will
perceive a faint shadow of the true Constellation and of the double dance which circulated
from the point at which I stood."   At other
times he does not fear to make the most realistic comparisons.   Of a soul which hides itself
in its own refulgence he says it is like " an animal wrapped in its own silk," a silk-worm in
cocoon; the soul of Adam is seen through his
coverings of light as the shape of an animal
can be discerned through a covering from which
it struggles to get free.

In addition to their literal and poetic meaning, these representations of light and song have
another, a doctrinal interpretation, which they
hold in common with the torments of the " Inferno " and punishments of the " Purgatorio."
But in this third portion of the " Comedy " the
two meanings are less distinctly separated and
tend in much greater degree to merge one into
the other.   His conception of the joy of Paradise limits the poet very closely, and the fact

that he is bound to one class of image, confines
the scheme of colouring to one tint, susceptible
of no alteration save changes in gradation to
lighter or darker. Only its spatial configura-
tion may alter very slightly by the use of specially chosen vocables and comparisons. It is
this which frequently arouses an impression in
the mind of the reader that many passages and
scenes are overcharged, that skill is exchanged
for effort, natural movement for gymnastic violence; and many readers, forgetful of the nature of true poetry, keep all their admiration for
these scenes of the " Paradiso," uttering praise
of questionable æsthetic taste. This not infre-
quent impression of poverty amidst profusion,
of void in plenty, of exuberant wealth which yet
is poor and has its origin in a certain poverty,
like the gloss of a covering varnish, is increased
by the intellectualistic (although ingenuously expressed) nature of the marvellous lights which
dispose themselves in wheels and crosses, or in
the shapes of roses and eagles, or in stairways,
or in letters forming Latin mottoes, and sententious admonitions. Negative hyperbole is
brought in quite naïvely as a means of heighten-
ing certain effects. Thus, all existing beauties
of nature or art avail nothing in comparison

with the " divine pleasure which dazzled me ";
or again, compared with the music of a certain
lute, the sweetest earthly melody " would seem
a crashing of thunder." By a trick of rhetoric
less efficacious, the poet protests that all he sees
and hears is indescribable and ineffable. At the
opening he says that in the empyrean he beheld
things " not possible to be recalled by one
freshly returned therefrom," and invokes not
only the " Parnassian yoke," which had sufficed
for the other two poems, and the aid of the
Muses, but " both of them," that is to say, the
aid of Apollo as well; at the close, he speaks
once more of having beheld that which is " too
vast for our speech." All through the " Paradiso " on every occasion, he repeats that were
he to summon all " talent, art and power " he
would still be unable to describe it " in any
imaginable manner "; that his " memory " over-
comes his " wit "; that his pen " skips " that
which he heard and " cannot write it " because
imagination does not " repeat it " and human
fancy, to say nothing of speech, is " too coarsely
coloured " to treat of such matters; and so on.
The light, the joy he wishes to think and represent is so pure, perfect and holy, so absolute,
that it is often converted into the abstract and,

as such, is impossible to imagine. It is only
possible to imagine concrete joy, born of grief
and destined to return to grief; or light which in
part is shade, fights against shade, conquers it
and, in part, is conquered by it.

On the other hand, as an inevitable consequence, the secondary, spiritual, or abstract
meaning is perpetually compromised by the
concrete images, which still retain their weight,
so to speak. In the midst of so much infinite
there is something too much of finite, which is
grotesque by very reason of the contrast between the intention and the performance. One
is aware of this, not only in the above quoted
illustrations of spectacular lights, which suggest
the motions of the heavenly bodies, or descriptions of fireworks, and in the extremes of comparing the soul to the silk-worm's cocoon, and
Adam to an animal " wrapped but struggling,"
but in all the comparisons, even in the noble and
charming. They derive from earth and earthly
objects, and while giving form to what they
seek to describe, they destroy its ideality,
thereby debasing and defiling it. This monotony, these repetitions of effects, this artifice
and puerility so harshly condemned when en-
countered in the " Paradiso," and which has

been the cause of so much shaking of the head over Dante's foolhardy and reprehensible audacity in striving to picture the impossible, is actually to be found in all three parts of the "Comedy," but is accentuated in the third owing to its faithful representation of the scene and the poet's voluntary obedience to the demands of "theological romance." It is only a mistaken criticism which attributes it to some defect peculiar to the subject-matter of the "Paradiso."

For this reason, the heavenly journey is seldom remembered or prized for its grand symbolical representations of light and song, which cost their author such labour of conception and are placed by him in the forefront of the poem, where they dazzle the sight and melt and confound themselves in the memory. The poem is really loved for some individual vision of beauty and happiness, for the landscapes or scraps of such landscapes which are to be found here and there. We prefer to leave to æsthetics and professional admirers of sublimity the business of falling into ecstasy over the "architectonic" beauty of the "Comedy" and of being frigidly exalted by the grandeur and fascination of this world of light and sound, whilst we search out some particular creations. As example we may take the light seen by the poet in the form of a river, a brilliance rushing like a stream " refulgent with splendour " between two banks deliciously " painted with marvellous spring." It is so full of life! Beholding it, we feel again that sense of pure vitality often observed already in many figures of the " Comedy," animating beings and landscapes whether infernal, crepuscular, or heavenly. In this case it is as suave, gentle and refreshing as can be desired by the senses of man; and it increases ever in delight: " From the stream a shower of living sparks rose to scatter themselves amongst the flowers, like rubies set in gold. Then, as though inebriated with the scent, they slipped once more into the river. . . ." Amongst the beautiful images in the " Paradiso " it is one of the most lovely; but by no means is it the only one.

Very often the poet pours his most distinctively beautiful poetry less fully into minutely described scenes than into the comparisons with which he illustrates them, dwelling on them and delighting in them, while he fashions them into the perfection of little lyrics. Indeed, the " Paradiso " is full of these. They are remembered when the occasion from which they spring

and the heavenly spectacle they illustrate are
alike forgotten.   Who recollects or loves the
monstrous eagle made of lights or souls, with
his talking or singing beak?   But everybody remembers " the lark wandering through the air,
singing at first, then falling silent, satiated of
her last sweetness."   Who recollects or troubles
to understand clearly the method by which sound
rose from the body to the neck, from the neck
to the beak of the eagle, when he calls to mind
the verse " I seemed to hear the murmur of a
stream trickling down from stone to stone?"
The heavenly sun which shines in glory, light-
ing thousands of lamps in the way our sun
lights stars, does not touch the heart; but the
comparison which accompanies it throws us into
a dream of mysterious and sacred beauty:
"When in the serene full moon, Diana smiles
among the eternal nymphs who paint the sky in
every deep recess."   The " incandescent lights "
stud the heights, giving proof of their adoration of the Virgin Mary; but the ostentatious
yearning of these lights or souls has not the
value of " the baby who stretches his arms towards the breast."   The three lights which are
the three apostles, Saints Peter, James and
John, stay their triple dance and speak no more;

but their cessation is less pleasing than the little picture of the sea contained in the simile, " As when, in order to avoid fatigue or peril, the oars which were in the water an instant previously are now all laid down at the whistle's sound." The glorious wheel of the beatified, with St. Thomas in it, turns and gives utterance to a voice sweeter than could be heard outside Paradise; but we are content to linger over the sweetness of the comparison of waking in the morning when the clock " urged and impelled by some of its wheels strikes *tin-tin* with so clear a note that the happily attuned spirit overflows with love." " A most clear splendour," which is St. John, separates itself from the company with whom it revolves and advances to join the two others; the dominant in this episode is neither the rising nor the departure of the most clear splendour, but the simile: " as arises and joins in the dance the happy maiden, solely to do honour to the newly married girl " . . . and the figure of Beatrice, standing amongst the dancers " like a bride, pallid and attentive." Examples could be multiplied, but are superfluous, for they are present to the mind of every reader.

The poetry penetrating and underlying the

entire scheme of the world of light is of such a
quality that we can contemptuously disregard
the vulgar judgment which denies the existence
of poetry in the " Paradiso," or holds that it is
poetry differing widely from that which precedes. All poetry presents individual variety.
But the poetry of the " Paradiso " has, as has
been pointed out, a physiognomy of its own. In
the " Inferno," fierce and bitter moods prevail;
in the " Purgatorio," the tender and humble; in
the " Paradiso " the joyous and ecstatic. The
accents of the last are not comparable with
those of the others; the critic, a new Paris,
knows not to which of the three he should
award the apple. There is no course open save
to inquire as has often been done or suggested,
to what sort of person, or at what time of life,
one poem appears more pleasing or appropriate.
But such investigations may be laid aside as
frivolous.

A different cast is given in the " Paradiso "
to the catalogue of souls. For the damned,
Lucifer led the rôle; for the souls in Purgatory,
Beatrice; for those in Paradise, Mary, Christ
and God. Since the passions described by us as
human die almost at the entry of Paradise, the
new catalogue cannot develop itself otherwise

than as a celebration of the "perfect" or of
those who have attained perfection; of sacred
doctors, apostles, defenders of the faith, wise
kings and well-intentioned emperors and so
forth; it is a series of encomiums. But encomium admits of little variety or amplitude.
This is evident in the " Paradiso," where name
follows upon name with always some mention
enabling someone to recognise it historically,
some record of work performed, some characteristic feature. Justinian is he who, inspired
by God, " from out the laws abolished the
superfluous and vain "; Gratian is the doctor
who " helped one and the other forum ";
Orosius is the " advocate of Christian days, the
Latin scribe appealed to by Augustine ";
Sigerius is a spirit " buried in deep thought,
grieving that his death should be so long de-
layed "; Gioachino, the abbot of Calabria, is
" gifted with the spirit of prophecy "; St. James
is " the Baron for whose sake Galicia on earth
is visited "; St. John, the evangelist, is " he who
lay upon our Pelican's breast " and from the
cross " received election to the great office ";
the haughty Harry is the emperor who " soon
shall govern and would guard Italy were she
not unprepared." In rare cases, as in those of

the two saints still fresh in history and memory, Francis and Dominic, encomium swells to panegyric: a panegyric delivered from a pulpit in the heavens by such holy orators as St. Thomas and St. Bonaventura.

These two are masterpieces of their kind, but it is useless to look for anything beyond the possibilities of their kind, beyond that which is permitted by the artificial requirements of pious encomium. After a preamble explaining the general significance of the office assigned by Providence to these two saints, the subject proposed for particular discussion, that of St. Francis, opens with a description of the birthplace of the saint, the fertile hillside hanging on a high mountain between the rivulets Tupino and Chiassi. This is a device seldom followed by the poet in the other poems but fairly frequent in the " Paradiso "; it arises sometimes from the necessities of historical information, more frequently from desire for external, oratorical flourish. The birth of the hero on this hill is spoken of metaphorically as the rising of the sun, with Assisi as the Orient. This metaphor is continued for a while, then is changed to one of a youth who rebels against his father and falls in love with a woman to whom nobody has ever opened the door of approbation, and the history of this woman or idea is traced through the ages; finally, when the attention of the listener has been secured through hyperbole and mystery and he is keenly eager to hear more, the names of the lovers are revealed—Francis and Poverty. He decribes their union as that of two persons happily married, in full accord and joyous amity. " Love and wonder and tender glances " were theirs amidst the holy thoughts they awakened in all beholders, and amid the sympathy which glowed at sight of this woman formerly despised, so that many threw off their shoes and raced after the bridegroom " so seductive was the bride." These are tricks of oratory. Then follow the chief events in the life of Francis; the journey performed with this woman and the unshod followers; the presentation of the humble brother's self to the pope, to whom he " royally " exposed his " hard intention "; the reiterated approbation of Honorius; the Christian faith preached by Francis in the presence of the proud Soldan; the retreat to the Verna; his death, when he recommended to his brethren " as to lawful inheritors " his most dear lady, commanding them to love her " in faithfulness," and died in her "lap," that is to say on the bare earth, directing he should be buried without a coffin. Even in this last, as is inevitable in oratory, images alternate without harmonising, striving by any means to attain their end, which, in panegyric, is devout edification. In like manner the panegyric of St. Dominic, after repetition of the opening, begins with a description of the birthplace of the hero, a description which is a mixture of the physical and the political, inspired by poetry (as are also many points in the earlier panegyric). The orator tells of a new espousal, wherein the bride is Faith, and extracts etymological significance from the name of the hero. This takes the shape of denunciation against the decadent and corrupt followers and modern representatives of the Franciscan and Dominican orders. The literary form of the panegyric develops into most noble prayer in the oration of the last canto, when St. Bernard with dignified humility prays the Virgin Mary to grant grace and strength to the mortal by his side.

If the catalogue of souls, reduced in the "Paradiso" to a series of encomiums, has few motives and narrow bounds, the doctrinal element, met with incidentally in the first two

poems, increases until it nearly fills the third
poem. Dante must have felt that Paradise is
not only the seat of infinite joy, but also of truth
and loftiest cogitation and doctrine, where
every difficulty disturbing the intellect shall be
removed and every obscurity made clear. He
was thus enabled to give free play to that which
had filled his mind to a great extent, urging him
to attend disputations between monks and professors, to read texts and interpretations, to
propound questions and solutions and himself
enter into argument. A great number of doctrinal explanations belonging to the theology
and philosophy, and to the physical, moral and
political science of his day, are scattered from
one end to the other of the poem. He discourses on the mode in which one rises to God
and holds that it is a spontaneous rapid movement when the soul is not weighted with a load
of imperfection; on the reason, not physical
but theological, of planetary spots; on the as-
signation of souls to particular regions of the
sky and the full enjoyment of beatitude in God;
on the symbolical location of souls in the
planets; on submission to violence, and the
shadow of responsibility which ever lies over
such submission; on the way in which vows may

be legitimately commuted; on the justice of Christ's death and the justice of vengeance against his executioners; on various natural dispositions of men ordained by divine will, and the crime of directing them to other ends; of the meaning of the supremacy of Solomon in knowledge vouchsafed to him as well as to Adam and Christ; on the resurrection of bodies and the increase of joy it will bring to the vision and fruition of God; on the inscrutable mystery of the damnation of the good who have not been baptised, and on predestination; on the orthodox definitions of Faith, Hope and Charity; on the earliest tongue spoken by man; on the First Cause, which is outside time and space and produces both; on the creation of angels and other substances; on the order of the blessed, and the place assigned to dead infants; and other doctrines and questions comprised or comprehended in these.

The treatment is didactic, as has been admitted, but it is still poetic and differs from any corresponding prose passages in that the dominating motive is not research or instruction but representation of the act of seeking or instructing. Dante leaves his prose of " De Monarchia," of " De Vulgari Eloquentia," and the

"Convivio," and soars to verse in the "Comedy," since form and poetry are more important to him, poet that he is, than matter, however powerfully this may appeal to him as philosopher, theologian, or politician. Here his doctrines are the libretto upon which he composes his music. As we observed in his first attempts at this kind of poetry, the teaching is placed in the scene and the action. This is specially noticeable in the "Paradiso," where we see Beatrice, St. Thomas, Solomon, St. Peter Damian, St. Bernard and others in turn filling the post of teacher. Throughout their discourse or lessons, we feel the movement in the spirit of the teacher, which introduces and develops concepts in the mind of the disciple. Step by step, the disciple is made to think like the teacher. For instance, take the discourse by Beatrice upon the cause of spots upon the moon. "Two cases are possible; this one is untenable, therefore we shall try to prove the other. If I disqualify that also you will see your conclusion is false." " Now that I have freed you from all error and have completed the negative part of my charge, I will fill you with so fierce a light that it will shower sparks around." Or take this passage, " Now look well, see how I go

through this towards the truth which you desire. . . ." One feels the satisfaction in the
mental order which arises and routs the disorder, and the joy of truth attained, radiating
splendour and composing itself into a picture.
The cause of moon-spots is discovered. It is
the Motive Intelligence which forges various
bonds between various planetary bodies, the
force deriving from joyous nature, " as a happy
vision makes the bright pupil flash."

Another instance:—St. Thomas has laid
down a couple of propositions and has read in
Dante's soul the difficulty and doubt with which
he is confronted and assailed. Having eluci-
dated the first, he goes on to the second, like
one who has accomplished one task and cheer-
fully undertakes another: " When one straw is
threshed, when its seed is deposed, sweet love
urges me to begin on another." At once he
sums up and consolidates what the learned
took to be true, and is true, then joining
it to his proposition, he brings into relief the apparent conflict resulting therefrom: " wherefore admire what I said before. . . ." Then follows exhortation to be
attentive and sharpen the mind so as to seize
the point of difficulty there where apparent con-

tradiction melts into real accord: "Now open
your eyes to what I am about to reply and you
will see your belief and my words show up, in
truth, like a central point in a circle." There is
development of the doctrine which is taken as
fundamental: "That which cannot die and that
which dies alike are radiance from the one idea
springing from love by order of our God." In
the first deduction there can be no possibility
of dispute, but if we stop here, we may reason-
ably raise an objection which exists already in
the pupil's mind; and that this may not occur,
the former saying must be completed by a distinction which makes everything clear and incon-
trovertible: "With this distinction, accept my
saying." The teacher proceeds to give his
pupil pedagogical warning that he venture
cautiously between affirmation and denial and
understand the necessity of distinguishing
clearly; that he hasten not to draw conclusions;
that he be on his guard against inclination and
self-love, which conduce to obstinacy in error,
into which he may have run in the first instance
through foolish precipitancy. The lengthy ad-
monition slides into a rambling record of the
thoughts and experiences of the speaker; history is drawn upon to fuurnish examples; finally

everything is concentrated upon a special case, the ill-considered judgment often passed upon the evil doing of such and such a person as to his salvation or perdition. In doing this, the poet runs rapidly over two scales. He is elevated in tone as he considers the almost miraculous power of good, together with the unexpected and tragic victory often gained, as he is forced to recognise, by the contrary power of evil. " I have seen a briar growing wild and untamed throughout the winter and later bear a rose upon its top: and I have seen a fair swift ship speed surely through her voyage and founder in the harbour." In abrupt transition he falls into the satirical, the familiar, the contemptuous: " Good country dame and honest yokel, do not suppose you have plumbed the depth of divine justice when you see one thieve and another make oblation." Dante knows the stimulus of doubt and the desire for truth, with the satisfaction of following it, and he describes this rhythm of the mind in lofty style: " Never can our craving mind be stilled save by truth . . . truth makes her way into the midst and lies crouching like a wild beast in its lair, and finds therein repose. . . ." From the truth our doubt shoots like sapling from root: " It is the work of nature lifting us from hill-top to hill-top." Admirable comparisons are found to illustrate the performance of those who act here as guide, teacher or listener. Such is the comparison of the bird, which, from the nest of its beloved young ones, "longing for daybreak perches on the bough," gazing with ardent desire towards the sunrise; and that other one of the "bough lately bent by the passing wind which lifts itself again, raised by its natural power."

In a group of explanations of doctrine near the end of the poem, there is a school-scene quite out of the ordinary. The pupil no longer stands humbly listening and begging for instruction but, being questioned, it is he who sets forth and expounds. Beatrice, who has hitherto taught and caused him to be taught, now presents her promising scholar to a great master, to him who was entrusted with the keys of heaven, to St. Peter; and she begs St. Peter to examine him upon the notion of Faith. Dante, who hears the request and sees the Saint consent, gathers his wits and arms himself with every argument, as though he were once again in the hall of a University: "as the Bachelor tries his armour, but is silent until his master propose his question, testing, not concluding." Once more we seem to catch a hint of that smile which has already lighted several scenes in the triple journey. The heavenly scene is indeed very human; an illustrious, most learned man, good-naturedly questions a boy on elementary subjects; kindly and good-humoured, St. Peter begins, " Now show us you are truly a Christian: What is Faith? " The boy, who is rather nervous, turns to her who is his teacher and she encourages him with her countenance " that I should pour forth the water gushing from my inmost fount." Every answer made by the good boy is approved and praised by the examiner, who follows every reply with a fresh question, in the hope that each will do him more credit, whilst the candidate rises gradually from timidity to confidence, from answers by rote to enthusiastic, personal eloquence: " This is the principle, this the spark, which kindles such a flame within, that like a star in heaven, I am on fire." Upon which, just as a lord embraces a servant who brings him glad tidings, St. Peter, the kindly examiner, girdles Dante thrice with his light and blesses him in song; and the candidate is very happy and satisfied with himself: " greatly had I pleased him with my sayings! "

The last canto shows us the exact opposite of this doctrinal and demonstrative proceeding; we reach intuition or vision of highest truth, of the reason of all things, of God, in which substance and accident, everything that is displayed in the universe, is bound and united. The poet cannot describe in logical terms what he sees, for it is ultra-logical; he cannot trace it as he saw it, for it flashed by in an instant, conceded to him through grace, then veiled in mystery. Nothing remains save the emotional residue felt for a moment, as after a dream remembered vaguely, but still disturbing: . . . " almost all my vision vanished, but in my heart yet lives the sweetness it distilled." Some trace of what he had seen lingers in the various vivacity of the pleasure he recalls: " I believe I saw the universal form of this knot, for in saying this I feel I enjoy more intensely." He repasses in tentative fashion over those things which his memory refuses to recall. His heart thrills at the accent of the manifold questions it asks itself, and replies with remembrance still vibrating with earlier joy.

Didactic poetry (or rather we should say "poetry of didactics") joins hands with oratorical poetry, which is strown through the third poem in the shape of deploration, invective and satire: Justinian recalls the history and glory of the imperial idea of Rome as a means of condemning at one blow both the Guelfs who oppose him and the Ghibellines who profess to follow him; Carlo Martello charges his brother, King Robert of Naples, with avarice and bad over-lordship; Cunizza foretells the punishments awaiting the populace of the Trevisan marches; Folchetto utters a denunciation against the cupidity of the clergy; the eagle accuses nearly every contemporary Christian ruler of vice and wickedness; St. Peter Damian inveighs against the luxury and corruption of the prelates, and St. Benedict against the decadence of Benedictine monks, as had St. Thomas and St. Bonaventura against Franciscans and Dominicans; St. Peter fulminates against the obscene slaughter his successors are carrying on in the church of Rome; Beatrice cries out against the loss of innocence and faith amongst men, owing to the lack of guidance, and later ridicules holy preachers and their shameless methods of buffoonery. Why should all this, mere oratory as it would be in other writers and versifiers, seem here to be poetry? Because it is the poetry of Dante's character, of his bitterness, his disdain, and of that expectation of vengeance and reward which shone in his soul like a star in the sky.

Invectives, satires, exclamations and imprecations gush out with vehemence, yet are always in perfect harmony. The images are most lifelike. The florin which Florence has coined, florin which symbolises the new economy centring there, is "the accursed flower," which has led astray sheep and lambs and converted their shepherds into ravenous wolves. Priests and monks are shown to be neglectful of the Gospel and the writings of the Holy Fathers, busied only in consulting and ransacking the volumes of Decretals, "as is seen by their edges," by their margins worn away with perpetual fingering at the pages. The prelates nourished in idleness and stifled in pleasures of the palate, "now must have supporters to prop their weight on either side, so gross are they, and to carry their train behind." Derision can go no further than in the poet's sketch: "they cover their palfreys with their cloaks, so that beneath one skin two beasts are hidden . . ."; or in that of the hooded friars who jump into pulpits and preach with mottoes and jokes, swelling with pride at the easy successes

they obtain: " they cause such a bird (the devil)
to rise behind their cowl that, could the vulgar
see it, they would soon learn what measure of
faith to place in pardons bought and sold." At
other times indignation prevails; when he sees
the spouse of Christ, the Church, nourished
with the blood of the early pontiffs (" with my
blood and that of Linus and Cletus ") now used
to gain money, while the highest keys are em-
blazoned on banners leading hosts to combat
against Christian peoples; or when he shudders
with horror when he notes how promptly the
corruption of the times destroys innocence, when
" the babe who listens lovingly to his mother "
is hardly grown but he " longs to see her in the
grave." The agonised soul breaks out " O
patience, what a load dost thou bear!" " O
God, our help, why dost thou delay? " But he
knows and calls to mind, as solace and comfort,
that Providence will not long delay to send
assistance; that the Vatican and all Roman territory, burying-ground of saints and martyrs,
will soon " be quit of the adulterer "; that " true
fruit must come after blossom."

The poetry, however, which may be called
" personal," whose material is supplied by the
personality and life of the poet, his firm convic-

tions, his expectations and hopes, has not only this one string of *indignatio*. Dante knew himself to be the depository and executor of a mission, he felt himself to be a poet, to be a prophet or, two in one, a poet-prophet, a poet-seer, whose voice should announce the truth and prepare mankind for judgment. He performs this mission with hope, consolation and dignity drawn from knowledge of his task. From the beginning of the " Paradiso " onward, Dante includes himself amongst the company of great poets, on the same plane with the company of great emperors and quite as limited, claiming for himself the laurel crown which the god of poetry must bestow on him, happy in the thought that many desire it and struggle with all their might to obtain it. Towards the close he dreams himself returned from exile, received back into his Florence, into the lovely fold where he had slept as a lamb. He is white-haired now, but girded with glory and crowned with the laurel-wreath at the very font where he had been baptised: acute nostalgia, tacit adjuration, consciousness of having deserved well, joy of recognition and triumph, palpitate in this dream of final reconciliation with men and things in which his weary soul must often have

found consolation. All his complexity of sentiment for his country, his love and pain, all his
life as citizen, urge him to erect a monument to
himself, and it is to be found in the middle of
the " Paradiso," in the episode of Cacciaguida.

Florence of long ago, but of a past not too remote, rises before him at this meeting, evoked
by the words of his earliest recorded ancestor.
Since Cacciaguida lived in the heroic and saintly
ages and was a crusader killed in battle against
the infidel, he speaks " not with modern speech "
but in sweet, archaic mode and in Latin. Sober
and austere Florence, simple and innocent in her
customs, is none other than the mirage of
Dante's ideal, the beautiful fiction of his desire.
He mistakes it for reality, a reality lost but in-
voked and capable of being restored. He be-
sieges his ancestor with enquiries as to the form
of the inhabited place of those days, about the
population, the leading families, and drinks in
particulars and names, the minutest of details,
like a loving searcher after memorials of his
birth-place, greedy for memories which speak to
the heart and revive the nobility and sacredness
of that past in which he replants his own root,
his own " nobility of blood," and rejoices himself therein. But ever and anon the ancient past

is shot through by its opposite, the new and modern. The city has spread beyond her first circle; the population has increased fivefold and has become mixed with ruffians and busy-bodies; merchants and bankers come and go through Florence, to and from every country in the world, and introduce fresh foreign customs; and there are many names of illustrious families either heard no longer or borne by poverty-stricken, much altered, members and descendants.

This conflict is the acknowledged cause of the drama of Dante's life as a citizen and the catastrophe in which it ended,—exile. It is this exile with its anguish of separation, its poverty and unfriendly and silly companions, its humiliations joined to the mitigations afforded by compassionate helpers, which is delineated broadly by a supersensitive soul, suffering every stab and almost weeping over itself (" Thou shalt leave everything that is most dear to thee . . . thou shalt learn how salt is the taste of another's bread . . ."); but he endures and bears it all, " a very tetragon against the blows of fate." He endures everything through that dignity which so preoccupied him,—through that hope, greater even than that other private and contingent hope of returning to his own town, the hope of immortality and glory, of the approbation and praise of future ages. Like all great men, he lives much more in the future than in the present, saying to himself, "And if I am a timid friend to truth, I fear to lose my life amongst those who will call these times ancient."

What is not found in the "Paradiso," because non-existent in the soul of Dante, is flight from the world, absolute refuge in God, asceticism. He has no wish to fly the world; he desires to instruct, correct and inform it, and bring it to the full completion of heavenly beatitude. No doubt he understood the beauty and joy of such a state, but he felt the world just as keenly in all its activity and passion. Not even in the empyrean and expressing his amazement at finding himself transported from the human to the divine, does he become unmindful of Florence. For him, humanity concentrates and individualises itself in Florentine society ("and from Florence [came] to people just and sane "). When the two worlds, heaven and earth, the divine and human, are brought together by him and enter into sharp conflict, it

cannot be said that the divine conquers entirely,
or completely and conclusively routs the other.
In the solar sphere St. Thomas shows him the
souls of the learned in divinity and calls to mind
their sublime speculations. The poet, ravished
by the lightning-rays and the sweet songs of
these spirits, is immediately struck by thought
of this earthly life. At this moment, whilst he
is standing by Beatrice, intent on celestial
glories and free from worldly tie, what is being
done by mankind, his equals? With his sight
he follows their doings down there on earth:
those who dispute in law-courts; those who
study medicine; those who become priests; those
who seek to overcome by means of force and
sophism; the thieves; the merchants; those who
lose themselves in carnal joys and idleness;—it
is a comprehensive record of the life of labour
and cupidity and pleasures of mankind. Moreover, although the poet calls these things " the
senseless cares of mortal man," the sentiment
underlying his verse is one of astonishment, as
at two worlds he can by no means reconcile.
What a strange thing is reality! On one side
the Heavens call us and circle round, showing
their eternal beauties; on the other, our eyes fix

themselves on earth and will not be drawn away
from that ardent, longing gaze. Ascending
still higher through the skies, he looks beyond
the seven spheres and perceives " this globe."
He sees it in such guise that he smiles at " its
ugly seeming."   Whilst with the " eternal
Twins " in the constellation of the Gemini, his
eye measures " the spot which makes us
so savage," all of it " from hill to sea-
shore," and turns at once his own eyes to
the beautiful eyes of Beatrice. But even here
his contempt is not wholly contempt; this
spot is his own as well, and he recognises it as
the house in which he dwells. " It makes us so
savage "; but it makes him savage too. It fills
all men with passionate vivacity. In the light
eternal it may seem a small and poor thing;
yet, small and poor though it be, it attracts with
powerful and mysterious force, the efficacity of
which is recognisable in every part of this poem
of his own composition. When once again he
looks toward the earth, he sees " beyond
Gades " the " mad flight of Ulysses," that Ulysses of whom he had sung in lofty strain, and it
seems that he is still stirred by the voluptuous
tale of old; and a little further away he de-
scries the place where the Phœnician maiden,

adored, desired, ravished, began her journey of
love on the back of the heavenly bull, the shore
" where Europa made herself a delicious
burden."

CHAPTER VII

THE CHARACTER AND UNITY OF DANTE'S POETRY

In this rapid passage through the three poems, no attempt has been made (and who would ever set himself such a task?) to establish the foundations of all the poetry of the "Comedy," that is, to describe it in every part. The intention has rather been to point out the various summits of the immense mountain-range, lest, owing to a lack of precise and particular detail in the mind of the reader, the characteristic quality of the poetical Dantean spirit, in which we have found the true unity of the poem to reside, be lost and disappear in a host of general considerations.

What is then this spirit of Dante, the "ethos" and "pathos" of the "Divine Comedy," its individual "quality"? It is, briefly, a view of the world founded on firm faith and steady judgment, and inspired by a strong will. Whatever be

the reality, Dante knows it; and no perplexity
will obstruct, divide, or weaken his knowledge,
which contains no mystery, beyond that to which
we bow in reverence, and which is one with the
conception of the mystery of creation itself,
providence, and divine will, revealed only in
the vision of God, in celestial beatitude. It may
sometimes have seemed to Dante that even this
mystery became less impenetrable at those moments in which he experienced or imagined
mystical ecstasies. Nevertheless, in his poetry
his mystical perception was translated, and had
to be translated, in negative fashion, into an
account of an experience of things ineffable. In
similar manner Dante knows how to judge
human emotions and how he should bear himself towards them, what acts he should approve
and perform, and what he should condemn and
repress, in order to bring his life to a true and
praiseworthy end. His will does not falter or
oscillate between discordant ideals; he is not
torn by desires dragging him in opposite directions. The inconsistencies and conflicts which
we can discover in his thought and attitude,
have their roots deep in the nature of things
themselves, developing in later history. In him
they exist only in germ, undeveloped and out-

side of his consciousness—a consciousness that is both compact and unitary. His faith is firm, and his behaviour consistent; he is sure both in thought and work. But set in this solid intellectual and moral framework, there is in Dante, as has been said, a very wide and complex conception of the world—the conception of a spirit that has observed, tried, and thought all things, that has had full experience of human vice and virtue—an experience gained not in a vague, easy, second-hand manner, but in direct contact and imaginative sympathy with life itself. The intellectual and ethical frame of Dante's thought holds and dominates this tumultuous experience, subjugating it entirely, albeit in the way a powerful adversary is subjugated and bound, an adversary who, whilst under the heel of the conqueror and with the chains binding his limbs, still strains his mighty muscles and draws them up in splendid lines.

The spiritual attitude we have just described is the only satisfactory explanation of the character of Dante's poetry. And indeed, how is it possible not to see, or to pretend not to see, what is so real, striking, and patent? Truth always reveals itself or, at least, shines through in many places. The formulas of Truth may,

however, strain the meaning and fail of their
intent if they are used for inadequate concepts,
or if they fall into metaphor, or lose themselves
in abstractions.   It is often remarked, for instance, that Dante draws not what is happening
but what has happened; not the present, but the
past.   What does this abstract distinction
amount to?   In Dante all the emotions are restrained, the particular is subjected to the universal; that is true enough.   But it is none the
less true that his powerful expression is, like
all poetry, a representation of movement, of the
kinetic rather than the static quality in things.
It is a common saying that Dante is supremely
" objective."   Yet no poetry is ever objective,
and Dante, as we know, is supremely subjective,
always himself.   Evidently " objectivity " is here
a vague metaphor for the absence of discord
in his conception of the world and his clear-cut
presentation.

It has also frequently been said that it is
Dante's custom to abolish all differences in time
and all diversity of customs, and to place men
and events of all ages on the same plane, which
is equivalent to saying that he measured all
earthly things by a single, undeviating rule, a
definite criterion of truth and goodness, that he

threw the transient on the screen of the eternal.
The characteristics of Dante's style have been
enumerated—his intensity, precision, concise-
ness, and so on. Certainly, he who by strength
of will is able to dominate strong passions
may be said to be both vigorous and intense
in expression; and, since he defines and
understands the passions, he is precise; and,
since he does not lose himself amongst their
details, he is concise. But to content oneself
with such an enumeration of characteristics is to go no further than the external. It is common also to call Dante a
" sculptor-poet " not a " painter." If by sculpture and the use of the chisel the critic means to
suggest a virile, vigorous, robust, and resolute
art in contradistinction to leisurely painting with
the " very light little brush " (to use Leonardo's phrase), Dante certainly is a sculptor,
not a painter. But it is futile to discuss the
imaginary parallels people are fond of drawing,
as, for example, the famous parallel between
Dante and Michelangelo.

A passage in the " Ottimo Comento " is well
known: " I, the writer, have heard Dante say
that no rhyme ever induced him to say anything
contrary to his purpose, but that often he made

words in his poetry express meanings differing
from those of other people." *Verba sequentur,*
and if they do not follow easily they are
dragged forth, as Montaigne said. Even the
assertion that the character and unity of Dante's
poetry are entirely in the metre in which the
poem is written—the terzina, linked, serried,
disciplined, vehement yet calm—is both true
and untrue; this must always be the case when
attempts are made to find the essence of an
art in its abstract form. These attempts are
much in vogue just now, especially in criticism
of the figurative arts. Undoubtedly the Dante
of the " Divine Comedy " was born in the
terzina; in it and through it alone he lived the
drama of his soul. But it is not possible that
the terzina (as is conjectured by some) should
have been consciously and deliberately chosen
by him as allegorical of the Trinity; if ever he
thought of such an allegory, the thought would
have merged itself with his soul's necessity, with
the spontaneous movement of his imaginative
expression with which the terzina harmonises—
the terzina as Dante wrote it, filled with qualities of diction, structure, and style that belong
to Dante alone, pulsating with the inflection and
accent given it by him, and quite different from

the terzina used by other poets.   Hence we come
to the obvious conclusion that the terzina is
referred to here, not as in itself the definition
of that particular poetry, but because it recalls
all the " ethos " and " pathos " of the " Divine
Comedy," its tone and quality, the spirit
of Dante.

That this spirit was an austere spirit, is in
conformity with the universal opinion of Dante
and is implied in one of his characteristics already mentioned, for he who bridles and sub-
dues passions is austere, and has within himself
a profound experience of pain. But when
fancy paints a Dante with his face perpetually
contorted with contempt, or when critics speak,
as they have spoken, of his " black humour," his
" misanthropy," his " pessimism," it is time to
utter a warning against exaggeration, and it will
not be amiss if we retouch and soften some of
the lines in the traditional and conventional portrait. Howsoever Dante may have appeared to
his contemporaries and passed into legendary
lore, even though his face were " pensive and
melancholy " as described by Boccaccio, it is
certain, as his poem proves, that he had a rich
variety of interests which led him to the past
away from the present, from the immediate

facts of life and suffering to the pleasant refuge
of learned and scholastic memories, and a richness and variety of emotions, from the most violent and sublime through the sweet and tender
down to the level of jest and laughter.

And he was a poet. Throughout the states of
Italy the eye of this exile did more than glance
politically and morally at things political and
moral; it ranged over every sort of spectacle,
delighting in the sights, turning with admiration
towards beautiful things and with sympathy towards the lowly. And besides being a poet,
Dante was specifically an artist: he studied art
perpetually; he theorised about it; he gloried
in his " beautiful style " and took great pleasure
in words, in appropriate, suitable, sensuous
speech, which is very thought giving birth, with
a divine throb of creation, to a living body. He
had a much wider range of emotions—above all,
far more gaiety—than is generally admitted,
although these emotions and this joy were
always framed by his habit of austerity, and
tempered and attuned thereto.

In Italy no less than in other countries, controversy rages round the " modernity " or
" non-modernity " of his spirit; which means, in
clearer terms, that we moderns should inquire

whether Dante can or cannot be taken as our
master and guide in spiritual life, political and
moral ideas, and everything else. Now, the
truth is that all great men are teachers in life;
but no one man may be the sole teacher, since
each is but a historical moment and the true
master is history itself—not alone that which
we are continually recreating but also, above all,
that which we are creating every instant.
Eternal in poetic form, in other respects, even
in its material, the " Divine Comedy " is limited
to the historic moment to which it owes its
birth—a moment which we have already briefly
sketched.   The historical study of its birth
teaches us to discriminate between what is found
in Dante that did not previously exist, and what
is not to be found, and could not be found, in
him, since it arose subsequently; and to remove
several colours and shadows which have been
clumsily laid on his portrait.

In Dante the Middle Ages, the cruel ages,
with their fierce asceticism or fierce and happy
warfare, no longer exist. Perhaps no other
great poem is so free as the " Divine Comedy "
from the passion for war as war, for the emotions that are part of military strife—danger,
violence, triumph, adventure. There is just a

faint echo of the mediæval epic of the Car-
lovingian period used as a metaphor in an oc-
casional terzina.   Instead of asceticism, we find
firm faith, reinforced by thought and doctrine;
instead of warlike, we have civil ardour, such as
belonged essentially to his age and country and
was reflected in his own concentrated and passionate spirit.

Although I have frequently expressed my
distaste and repugnance for ethnical charac-
terisations of poets, I will say that if the epithet "Germanic," which has been thrust on
Dante (not by Germans alone, or by Germans
in the first instance), is to be taken as symbolic
either of mystic or ascetic bias or of warlike
propensities, Dante was not "Germanic."   He
should be accounted Italian or Latin, or something equally opposite.   In the fine description
by Giovanni Berchet in his "Fantasie" of the
meeting of Italians and Germans at Constance
for the negotiation of peace, Dante would have
no place amongst "the fair-haired folk" and
the barons who, with iron helmets and breasts
cased in iron coats of mail, "appear as signs of
a bygone day," but he would stand in the group
wrapped in long plain capes "conspicuous only
by the earnest gaze of their black eyes."

For other reasons, we must avoid making too rigorous a comparison between Dante and Shakespeare, the first equally great poet with whom we meet after Dante in the history of European poetry. Shakespeare represents, and is, another epoch of the human spirit, in which Dante's conception of the world was overturned, and in which a fresh veil of mystery was drawn over the brightness that in Dante's time still illuminated even the necessity for mystery—an epoch in which a perplexity of mind and soul that Dante either had not known or had quickly vanquished, became the dominant note.[1]

What is one to say of Dante and the romantics who followed him? Their infinite is not his; their dreams are not his; their style is not his *bello stile;* their "feeling for nature" (which Grimm refuses to acknowledge in Dante) is not his; and in general, their outlook on life is the exact opposite of his. Had he been acquainted with the heroes of the romantic school—Werther, Obermann, and René, with their pallid brethren—it is possible he might have put them in the "black slime" among the

[1] See my essay "Shakespeare," in the volume "Ariosto, Shakespeare, and Corneille, Bari, 1920, translated into English by Douglas Ainslie, New York, 1921, Henry Holt and Company, and London, 1921, George Allen and Unwin.

sluggards. He must have known something of this sad state of mind which the romantic period delighted especially to enrich, to complicate, to prolong, and to carry to an apotheosis of admiration, but which is common in all times. Perhaps he himself, when a youth, suffered from this disease, and, like the romantic heroes, through melancholy, sadness, and idleness, allowed himself to drift into dissipations. This may have been the cause of the sonnet addressed to him by his friend Cavalcanti reproving him for the " vile life " in which he " indulged," for the " baseness of soul " and the " spirit of evil " which had taken possession of him. In any case, he quickly rid himself of these irregularities and put them amongst his other experiences, along with those furious love passages mentioned by his biographers, to be drawn upon when he wrote the Francesca episode. In the " Divine Comedy " there is no sentimentalism of any kind, only joy and grief and the courage of life, curbed by moral restraint, sustained and animated by high hope.

Such, in rapid strokes, is the portrait of Dante, the authentic portrait, taken from his own writings. But it must never be forgotten that this picture which serves to differentiate

Dante from other poets and helps towards an intelligent understanding of his works becomes, in common with all characterisation, narrow and, so to speak, prosaic, if it be not set in the fulness of poetry—poetry alone, which never imprisons itself in any one thing or group of things, but spreads itself throughout the cosmos. It is the cause of our delight in the rhythm and words of Dante, even the slight, fugitive words, which come toward us filled with enchantment: whether he calls the dawn mythologically "mistress of ancient Tithonus" rising "from the arms of her sweet friend," or calls the snow "white sister." This is the essential, which cannot be described otherwise than as universal poetry. From this point of view Dante is no longer Dante as a definite individual, but is that marvelling and impassioned voice which the human soul transmits from age to age in the ever recurring creation of the world. At this point, all differences vanish, the eternal and sublime burden of the song alone resounds— which has the same fundamental quality in all great poets and artists, always new, always old, received by us with ever-renewed trembling and joy: Poetry without any adjective. Those who spoke in such divine, or, rather in such profoundly human, accents, were given the name of Genius in former days; and Dante was a Genius.

CHAPTER VIII

HISTORICAL SURVEY OF DANTEAN CRITICISM

If we examine in chronological order all that was written about Dante, from the days of the poet himself until we reach the pages written by Giovanni Battista Vico about 1725, we become aware (supposing we can appreciate such things) that these last inaugurate nothing less than a revolution in Dantean criticism.

At Vico's solemn words, the figure of Dante seems to rise suddenly, towering over the land of Italy. Dante (says Vico) is a divine poet, entirely different from the erotic, honied, Arcadian, present-day versifiers. His poetry springs from the greatness of his soul, which scorns all things dear to greedy, effeminate men, and desires immortality alone, aflame with public-minded, noble virtues, especially magnanimity and justice; it comes, too, at a peculiarly favourable moment of history, at the beginning of a long age of violent passions and fervid imagination, in the days of expiring barbarian rule in

Italy.   Regarded in this light, his poetry can be compared with none save that of Homer; for truly Dante was the Homer of the Middle Ages, writing his " Iliad " in the " Inferno " and his " Odyssey " in the other two poems, the " Purgatorio," where suffering is borne with admirable patience, and the " Paradiso," where infinite joy awaits the soul which has entered into the beatitude of peace.   Of him, as of Homer, it was said that by the miracle of his art he had fashioned his own language, selecting it from amongst all the dialects of his nation. The " Comedy " must be considered from three points of view: that of literary study, in connection with the great beauty attained by use of the Tuscan idiom; that of history, since it comprises a history of the barbarous days of Italy; and, greatly more important, from that of poetry, since it is in itself an example of all that is sublime in poetry.   It is poetry which springs entirely from vigour of imagination; and although it has become customary to praise Dante for his great erudition in theology, the fact is that this doctrine, this philosophical and theological science, are to his disadvantage rather than in his favour, for " had he been ignorant of Latin and scholastic philosophy, he

would have been even greater as a poet, and
perhaps the Tuscan tongue would have served
to make Homer's equal," a result not achieved
even by Virgil, the most cultured of scholars.
The correct way of commenting on Dante is
to give a concise and clear account of the things,
facts and persons he describes, and explain his
sentiments by " entering into the spirit of what
he wished to say," in order to comprehend the
beauty of his poetic utterance, " putting on one
side all moral, and, much more, all scientific
knowledge." [1]

Dante had never been considered in such
wise before. We do not mean to say, of course,
that the author of the sacred poem had not
been received and generally proclaimed as a
poet, and a great poet, or that his peculiar physiognomy had not been noted and recognised;
the admiration he began to excite even amongst
his contemporaries, the chapter which Giovanni
Villani devoted to him in his " Cronica " (as one

[1] See *Scienza nuova* (1725), b. III. c. 26; *Scienza nuova
seconda,* ed. Nicolini, pp. 477, 727, 733, 734, 750; the letter
to Degli Angioli of December 26, 1725, and the *Giudizio sul
Dante,* written on the occasion of a new commentary on the
Commedia which appeared in 1728 or 29 (for this date see
Critica XVI, 156). See also Croce, *La filosofia di G. B. Vico*
Bari, 1911, c. XVIII. English Translation by Collingwood.
(London, George Allen and Unwin.)

of the marvels of the age), the public readings, the numerous comments, the imitations, the method and tone of the discussions the poem aroused in its own day and throughout the three succeeding centuries, the very controversies which sprang up around it, all testify to the fact that whenever the minds of men came into contact with Dante, they invariably acknowledged the grandeur and originality of his severe genius. Nor is it of the least importance, for that matter, that certain men, or whole generations, should have neglected or abjured him, especially in the humanistic period, and later in the time of Bembo or, later still, during the baroque era of the seventeenth and the rationalistic period of the eighteenth centuries; vicissitudes of this nature befall all the works of man, according to the various interests, practical, mental or even artistic, which dominate various individuals in different ages. Further than this, even when such works are known and admired and rightly estimated, there still remains the necessity to demonstrate and to regulate the judgment, as well as to support and determine it theoretically; by which act alone it can become critical and scientific. To this end, it is necessary to have a theory. Now, the theories in vogue during these centuries, orig-inated in Greco-Roman times, and, variously intellectualistic as they were, did not permit free treatment of poetic problems; whether it was through these theories that justification was sought, or whether judgment more or less ad-verse was passed on the works of Dante, the method employed was, of necessity, artificial.

Notwithstanding his acute appreciation of the nature of poetry, evidenced in many passages of his writing (as, for example, when he says his poetry is written " just as the inner spirit dictates "; and again when he scouts the pos-sibility of translating into another language ex-pressions which are united metrically), Dante himself was strictly bound by the doctrine that poetry must exist primarily in the sense of alle-gory conveying religious or moral truth; nor can that which he calls " literal meaning," plac-ing it as basis for the other three, be taken as representing our " poetical meaning," for that would be rather poetry deprived of potential virtue, perceived in a superficial manner only, and agreeable by reason of its gleaming surface. Certainly he was not unconscious of his power of creation, for he was fully sensible of his force and dignity as poet; but his scholastic philosophy prevented him from adequately understanding his own poem in the category to which it belonged. In the same way, Boccaccio held theology and poetry to be substantially identical, one was the poetry of God, the other employed lovely words to show forth the reasons of things, the effects of virtues and admonitions which philosophical demonstrations and oratorical persuasions could not bring home to the souls of men. Giovanni Villani had praised the " Comedy " more simply, saying it was composed " in elegant rhyme, treating of great and subtle moral, natural, astrological, philosophical and theological questions, with beautiful new figures, comparisons and poetics." He was filled with admiration at the universality of Dante's learning, " The most universal of men," as he is called by Antonio Pucci. In the following century, inspired perhaps by certain Platonic dicta, Leonardo Aretino proclaimed another species of poet as the highest and most perfect of the kind, those poets, namely, who compose " through innate talent agitated and moved by a certain internal hidden force called fury or mental possession." These are placed by him above those who compose " through science, through study, through discipline, art and prudence," among whom he did not hesitate to assign Dante a place, for "by studying philosophy, many different books, vigilantly sweating over his studies, he acquired science, subsequently adorning and explaining it in his verse." During the sixteenth century the revival of the poetic of Aristotle did nothing to eradicate the didactic, oratorical view of poetry. The study of the works of this philosopher, and of the ancient rhetoricians, led to the construction of a rigid classification of legitimate styles of poetry, giving rise to one of the gravest controversies about Dante: must his " Comedy " be regarded as epic or dramatic, or some other kind? Jacopo Mazzoni, for instance, opposed the general opinion that the poem was epic and pronounced it to be dramatic,—" comedy in no way ridiculous " and not unknown to the ancients, with Dante as protagonist, Virgil as deuteragonist and Beatrice as trisagonist. On the other hand Jason de Nores held it to be a theological or philosophical morality in verse, comparing it with the poems of Empedocles and Lucretius. These disputes were prolonged throughout succeeding centuries, when some defined it as a " satire," whilst others, such as Monti, defined it as didactic. Some again, as Francesco Torti, an enemy of Monti's, pronounced it an epic, inasmuch as it is a " narrative of an illustrious action "; others, as Becelli in 1732, found it a medley of all styles of poetry, " now tragic, now comic, often satirical and yet again lyric and elegiac." This last definition met with great favour, or rather it revives spontaneously, and we meet it again in Schelling (who speaks of the " Comedy " as " not didactic, strictly speaking not romance, not comedy or drama, but an indissoluble mixture, a perfect interpenetration of all these things "; an entity in its own peculiar style, a world in itself " calling for its own especial theory "). It is even frequently met with in critical articles of our own day, since it furnishes easy means for evasion.

Putting aside such disputes of empty formalism, the course of the sixteenth century saw the " Comedy " praised by many who, like Varchi, started from the above-mentioned doctrine of the didactic-oratorical nature of poetry, and praised Dante for the pursuit of a high moral aim in punishing the wicked with pains of Hell and rewarding the good with joys of Paradise. He was blamed by others who clung to an ideal of sensuously delightful poetry and agreed with Muzio's declaration that he "was everything but a poet." His poem was even condemned as hard dry versification, and he was accused of having written it on some few quires of paper given him by theologising, argumentative monks. It comes as a pleasant surprise when, having read and re-read the documents concerning this sixteenth century controversy (many of them connected with the diatribe launched against Dante in 1571 by a person calling himself Rodolfo Castravilla), we come across some words of Vincenzo Borghini loudly rejecting the censures of sensual voluptuaries and the praises of didactic partisans. To the former class, who pretend to draw their inspiration from Bembo, Borghini mildly observed that the famous Venetian man-of-letters " directed by his genius towards a different style of poetry, sweeter, perhaps, and more delicate, neither enjoyed nor studied that other style in such a way as to be able to judge of it correctly." To those who held themselves bound to admire Dante " for the number of wise sayings to be found in the poem," he remarked that it would indeed be foolish to overlook such things, but (he added) " I declare that I hold them as adjuncts, not principals, of the poem. I admire the poet him-

self so much as poet, and not as philosopher or
theologian, that it seems to me a kind of divine
genius to have used these things with grace and
charm according to the needs of the poem. If
Cosmico sees no more in Dante's poem than
what he says about it—and he has very little
taste for it—I say it would be better if he spent
his time in reading some other book." [1] Borghini had invented an excellent system for research into Dantean language and just insight
into the poetical characteristics of Dante; nevertheless his teaching fell flat without finding an
echo either in his hearers or in himself, because,
in order to make it cogent and effective, he
would have had to make open war upon the
entire poetic of the time,—a course he did
not adopt.[2]

The value of Vico's judgment, on the other
hand, lies in its embodiment of a new doctrine of
poetry, suggested by Dante and Homer and

[1] "Studii sulla Divina Commedia," by G. Galilei, V.
Borghini and others, ed. Gigli (Florence, 1855), p. 308.

[2] Concerning which objections were raised as soon as the
Scienza nuova began to be studied a century later; see
Fauriel, *Dante et les origines de la langue et de la littéra-
ture italienne* (Paris, 1834), I. pp. 21-2, pp. 371-3; Villemain,
Tableau de la littérature au moyen age (Paris, ed., 1882),
I. pp. 346-7. P. Emiliani Giudici. *Storia della letteratura
ital.* (4th ed., Florence, 1865), I. p. 228.

all great poets in their creations and, at the same time, accounting for them; a new doctrine, to be developed in succeeding centuries and named æsthetic, science of the imagination, science of intuition, and such like. In face of this great merit, what can it matter if Vico did strain the comparison between Dante and Homer, between the Italy of the twelfth century and the Hellas of the ninth century before the Christian era, or if he exaggerated the dependence of poetry upon the barbarous ages of society and thought for a moment of denying Dante one part of his mind, the scholastic and Latin? Such things are concepts and devices to be considered with discretion; symbols rather than affirmations of fact; symbols, that is to say, of true poetry, which issues from passion not from reflection. What can it matter that he did not penetrate more deeply into the particular characteristic of Dante's poem, or enjoy every scrap of fruit to be gathered from the profound rules he had laid down for the method of interpreting the " Comedy "? All came later, and will have still further development in time to come; but the later steps could not have been made without the first.

We may say, then, that Vico's century saw

unfavourable judgment of Dante reach an extreme degree under the influence of an external ideal, the classicism and Bemboism of the sixteenth century which garbed itself afresh in rationalism. Literature was either reflective, satirical, gallant and sentimental, or " sensitive." Voltaire, who described the " Comedy " as a fantastic poem, not devoid of certain glowing natural beauties, but on the whole a confused mixture, a *salmigondis,* ridiculed the anachronisms it contained, and concluded his judgment with the sarcasm that its reputation would always be assured, since it was admired by all and read by none. Bettinelli also, making an exception of some short passages of about a thousand lines altogether, pronounced it a medley of sermons, dialogues, and disputes, guided solely by the caprice and inclination of the author; without action, or only such as is derived from descents, walks, ascensions, comings and goings; bristling with symbols and full of allusions to obscure individuals, contemporaries of the poet. These two were the most celebrated exponents of an opinion most generally received in their day. There were a great many sharers of their view; for example, Cesarotti, for whom the " Comedy " is a " grotesque farrago " an "un-divine Comedy," and, epigrammatically, Horace Walpole (1782), who called Dante "extravagant, absurd, disgusting, in short a methodist in Bedlam." An echo of this is found in Goethe who, in 1788, writes that he cannot understand how any one can find entertainment in the poem. The "Inferno" appeared to him horrible, the "Purgatorio" equivocal, and the "Paradiso" tiresome. Such anti-historical sentiments like those as to the literary "classes," were not confined to the eighteenth century, nor are they wholly unknown nowadays. Lamartine repeats Voltaire and Bettinelli when he calls the "Comedy" that "*Gazette florentine,*" a polemic which "*la posterité ne comprend plus.*" An American critic also returns to the charge, declaring that in the confused mass of extravagance and disorder he can discern nothing save "several literary jewels," "a very small residuum." [1]

Answers to such criticisms were often dictated by simple good sense in the eighteenth century (as for example when Bettinelli was informed that Dante has no obscurity for men of culture, and Gasparo Gozzi taught that the

[1] Mordell, *Dante and Other Waning Classics* (Philadelphia, 1915).

way to understand Dante was to study the times in which he had lived and the other books he had written) ; unfortunately, at other times they took the form of a false defence in opposition to false accusations, of old pedantries opposed to new, such as praising him for " gravity " of thought and morals, and for having been the first to " open a glorious path for the poetry of Italy." Still, one was found to make answer in what may be called the spirit of Vico, a German writer, either Bodmer himself or one of his friends or pupils, who wrote in the *Zurich Review* of 1763 an anonymous article which was forgotten for a very long time.[1] The writer began by saying that Dante's extraordinary poem shared in the accusations against the " Iliad," as being contrary to propriety, to decency, to the delicacy of modern taste, unmindful of rules and unity of action; but Dante (he insisted) did not fail to observe the rules he laid down for himself, providing so many great and strange subjects for his pen that, in order to

---

[1] It was discovered and reprinted by my lamented friend Leone Donati in his monograph *J. J. Bodmer and die ital. Litteratur* (in vol. *J. J. Bodmer: Denkschrift zum CC Geburtstag, Zürich,* 1900, pp. 283-288): it seemed to me sufficiently important for translation and insertion in *Critica* XVIII, pp. 306-11.

show his command over every style of poetry, no better form could possibly be adopted than that of an imaginary journey. Those parts of the poem which were condemned as unusual, Gothic, contradictory or affected, might, with as great a show of justice, be described instead as singular and original; and the author of the " Comedy " had as much right to write poetry in the style of his time as we have to write in the style of our own. This acute critic, moreover, justified Dante on historical grounds for the freedom with which he treated ancient mythology and introduced exceptions to the laws governing the other world. He praised him also for seeking poetry not in human passions alone, as in the love of Francesca and the martyrdom of Ugolino, according to ideas pleasing to modern taste, but also in morality and theology, which he rendered poetical by his art.

When people chatter about the uselessness of criticism, they do not remember that, if we are now able to read Dante and other poets without encountering obstacles interposed by the gross prejudices of former days, this facility and benefit are due entirely to critics such as we are discussing; it is they who have liberated, or are liberating us. In the generation following Bodmer, through the effect of new ideas about poetry and history springing, for the most part, as blossom or harvest from seed sown by the hand of some isolated individual, anti-dogmatic and historical consideration of Dante and other poets became usual and a matter of course; on every side was found contempt for judgments dictated by sectarian, eighteenth century illuministic taste, or for what was not in accord with the true and intrinsic ideal proper to Dante himself and to the age in which he lived. This is shown clearly in the characteristics of Dante invariably given in general histories, histories of literature and philosophies of history, where a more or less successful attempt is made to portray the author of the " Comedy " as representative of an historical era. In Italy, Dantean criticism, which was a labour of erudition amongst the learned men of the eighteenth century, becomes pre-eminently historic when treated by Foscolo at the beginning of the nineteenth century. Wilhelm Schlegel wrote, " an orthodox critic of taste thinks he has said everything, when he judges the ' Divine Comedy,' the ' Universal Justice ' and ' Macbeth ' to be without taste; in saying this he expresses nothing beyond the fact that he cannot

understand these works, that they extend beyond the horizon of rules and conventions
familiar to him." And more particularly in regard to the " Comedy," he says, " For this, one
must know how to conjure up a vision of that
heroic and monastic epoch of strife, with its
Guelfs and its Ghibellines; otherwise one
throws the book down as tiresome." Although
Goethe never attained to a profound knowledge
of Dante, he came to understand and consider
him in a way very different from that he had
adopted in 1788, and in a letter of 1826, he
associates him with the revival of figurative arts
in Italy, for in Dante " as in Giotto, predomi-
nated sensible, figurative genius by which he perceived objects so clearly with the eye of fancy
that he was able to give them distinct form, and
to outline the most occult and marvellous as
though they stood before him in reality." In
conversations with Eckermann he spoke of him
not simply as a " talent " but as a " nature."
Dante was now placed among new and lofty
companions. Critics of the sixteenth century
compared him with Homer (calling forth loud
protests, as in the case of Varchi),—Vico himself had insufficient acquaintance with foreign
literature to enable him to make other com-

parisons. The English of the eighteenth century likened him to Milton on account of a certain similarity of matter; and an Italian of the name of Rolli, living in England in 1735, for the first time linked the name of Dante with Shakespeare. The triad, Homer, Dante, Shakespeare, was now soon formed, altered sometimes to include one or other of the three great modern poets by substituting the name of Goethe [1] for that of Homer, or, as recorded by Tieck,[2] altered to include those of the three chief masters of modern art, Dante, Cervantes, Shakespeare. Criticism of poetry was converted into history, into grand history, the history of the human soul. Nevertheless this justifiable reaction and noteworthy progress against and beyond the dogmatic criticism of preceding centuries was not without danger of being onesided; for, whereas ancient dogmatic criticism, even though its method were arbitrary and predetermined, was always artistic criticism,

---

[1] Toynbee, *Dante in English Literature,* I. p. 632, refers to the description of a journey in Germany made by H. Crabbe-Robinson in 1802:—"Our polite host placed me by the side of Professor Abicht, and I was again struck by the concurrence of opinion among the German philosophers as to the transcendent genius of Shakespeare, Goethe and Dante."

[2] In a fantastic play, reprinted in Del Balzo, *Poesie di mille autori intorno a Dante,* VII., pp. 421-52.

the new criticism, rightly taking to history, frequently lost sight of art as art, and, failed to become, as should have been the case, historico-artistic.   This is the reason why in recent times it has been necessary to reconstitute the history of poetry and of art with a sort of synthesis of the abstract æsthetic criticism of dogmatic writers and the abstract historic criticism of historical writers, incorporated in an æsthetic and, at the same time, historic treatment, the historico-æsthetic.[1]

It follows, therefore, that the attention of those who are interested in the progress of historical interpretation of Dante should not be directed primarily to enquiry into the intellectual signification of Dante in universal history (instituted with the intention of extending and enlarging the interpretation we have named " allotrious "). They should seek to discover the essential quality of historical interpretation itself, and its subsequent influence on the character of Dantean art, and on the historic-æsthetic researches which are usually accorded such scanty and confused notice. The majority of " Danteists " will marvel, consequently, at the

[1] See my *Nuovi saggi di Estetica,* pp. 161-184; also pp. 214-5.

number of books we are going to pass over in
silence; and that those we quote should be unknown to them, or, if not quite unknown, then
either not read or not appreciated, will cause
them equal wonder. Certainly we do not learn
much on the subject from Schelling, to whom we
owe the comparison, oft-repeated, of the " Comedy " with " Faust," and the remark that the
Dantean poem first manifested what belongs
particularly to modern poetry, a union of science, religion and art with history, and of history with allegory, and created a new mythology, so that it must be considered, not as a
single poem, but as " poetry of poetry." [1]
Hegel's definition of the " Comedy " (" a kind
of epic, having as its object eternal action,
eternal love "), followed shortly, bringing into
relief the treatment of actions and personages
which, with Dante, are invariably " judged."
High value should be set on the criticism of
Dante by Bouterweck (1801) [2] unaccountably
overlooked by students or, more unaccountably,
recollected through a vague accusation of mis-

---

[1] In *Philosophie der Kunst* (1802-3), and in the essay
Dante in philosophischer Beziehung.

[2] F. Bouterweck, *Geschichte der Poesie und Beredsamkeit
seit dem Ende des dreizehnten Jahrhunderts* (Gottingen,
1801), vol. I., pp. 76-120.

conception, detraction and calumny, or simply of being a continuation of Voltairianism and the irreverent spirit of the eighteenth century. There is no denying that Bouterweck is harshly critical of the " composition " or " construction " of the poem; it seems difficult to him to " save its honour "; it puts him in mind of a vast Gothic labyrinth, thick with clouds of allegory; a labyrinth which puzzles the mind and, in the end, does not compensate for the time and toil spent in trying to understand the architectonic and the conjoined regulation of punishments, purgations and prizes. The artistic sense (*das Kunstgefühl*) finds little or nothing in the groundwork of the " Comedy." The impossibility of dealing simultaneously with allegorical and literal sense had forced the author to omit and to subtilise; the unity of the work was spoiled, so that its external unity was little else than that of the story of a journey, not the internal unity of an epic and, as to the remainder, an allegorical or theological unity. He held the scholastic, theological and astronomical parts to be unpoetical, and the conception of the " Paradiso " of such nature that imagination was necessarily brought face to face with the inexpressible, the poetic void filled with the sole

element allowable even by dogma, light. The
" Comedy " therefore seemed to him " a gallery
of pictures in a grotesque frame." Yet, notwithstanding these defects of composition and
execution, " if it be examined in detail "*(wenn
wir sie fragmentarisch schätzen)*, the work is
" one of the most noble and beautiful produc-
tions of an original mind," a work in no way
prepared for by pre-existent literature, not deriving from any books read by the author and,
in this respect, unrivalled in modern poetry
without any exception whatever, for even
Shakespeare emerges from a crowd of predecessors; but not so Dante. This was attacking
the heart of the problem, and the acumen and
courage with which Bouterweck strove to distinguish between groundwork and poetry in
Dante and exalted the poetry above the groundwork should make us indulgent towards the
over-impatient treatment of the doctrinal elements of the poem, and the " fragmentary "
principle which, if it were in agreement on one
side with judgments passed on Dante by Bettinelli and other eighteenth century writers, on
the other was an anticipation of a freer method
of interpreting and admiring poetry.

This more liberal method was frequently fol-

lowed by critics of the first half of the eighteenth century; in Italy, besides Foscolo already
quoted, Leopardi, who held lyrical poetry in
higher estimation than any other kind, was
obliged to admit what he felt to be the truth,
saying in one of his shorter works, that the
" Comedy " is nothing but a long lyric, wherein
the poet and his own personal affections always
occupy the field.[1]   The same is true of the
Catholic, moralistic, sometimes grammatical,
Tommaseo.   In France, in his lecture-courses of
1833 and 1834, Fauriel said that the double
quality of man of science and poet was peculiar
to Dante among all great poets, and was the
cause of a kind of strife between the various
faculties observable in him.   For this reason,
his poem is lacking in the characteristic of unity,
being a mixture of poetry, science and politics,
although a certain unity pervades it, arising
from a sentiment running through it from beginning to end, a thought of love, the love of
Beatrice.   Fauriel, also correctly, swept aside
the allegories, in order to discover only
the poetic meaning of the representations; he
dismissed the censures, dictated by " abstract
taste and logic," upon the pagan figures intro-

[1] *Pensieri di varia filosofia e bella letteratura,* VII, p. 351.

duced by Dante into the Christian Hell, and
called attention to the sincerity of the poet in
transforming these figures into Christians.
He drew a distinction between history, which
was Dante's starting point, and the creations of
sentiment and imagination worked in upon its
background, as in the episodes, for instance, of
Francesca, Ugolino and Sordello. With no less
shrewdness did Villemain (1840) return to the
comparison with Homer in order to re-temper
it by emphasising the difference between times
and genius. He declared afresh that Dante,
divested of mediæval doctoral robes, created
" comme aux premiers jours du monde," and
spoke with *" la voix jeune et argentine du poète
grec "*; he was the first, or among the first, to
find the genius of Dante *" rêveur, triste, exalté,"*
un-Italian, meriting the title, were he *" moins
naturel,"* of Germanic. Recognising with
Fauriel, the double inspiration of the poem,
*" l'une instinctive et passionnée et l'autre
studieuse et scholastique,"* he found in it the reason for the sublime beauties of the poem as well
as for the extraneous details of great interest
to contemporaries if tedious to modern ears.
He concluded that *" ses fautes, ses inégalités, ne
semblent pas altérer l'originalité puissante et*

*continue de son style," " le génie de l'expres-
sion,"* in him so admirable, because he wrote
always *" avec la même inspiration de verve et
d'amour."* In England, Coleridge [1] saw in
Dante the " combination of poetry with doctrine, which is one of the characteristics of
Christian poetry," although it seemed to him
that Dante had not been so successful as Milton
in perfecting the union. On the other hand he
admired " the vivacity, the logical connection,
the vigour and energy " of Dante's expression,
which exceeded that of every other poet, Milton
not excepted, and his picturesque style, unrivalled amongst ancient and modern, recalling
the severe Pindaric style more than any other;
nor does it escape him that Dante had artistic
delight in language, in beautiful and efficient
speech. Without knowing it, Carlyle gave logical development to a thought of Vico's, when
he declared the " central quality " of Dante,
from which all other qualities flow as from a
common fount, to be his " greatness of heart."
He recognised his narrow partisanship in matters of faith; yet, notwithstanding this, held him

[1] Reference to Coleridge and other Englishmen mentioned below can be found in Toynbee, already quoted. See
p. 273.

to be profound; not " world-wide " but " world-deep." Hence his " abrupt precision," his utterance of a " smiting word," followed by silence. Carlyle felt the continuous-flowing melody of him, the " canto-fermo." Macaulay noted his melancholy, and that all love had fled from him save the half mystical passion for his dead Beatrice, its place being taken by a misanthropy so deep that " the ferocious and uneasy exile, even when in Paradise amongst the blessed, cannot be happy or participate in their joy." He regretted the importance attached by commentators to the physics, metaphysics and theology of Dante, all bad in their way, and to the allegories, to which they gave interpretations never intended by the author, whereas " the grand faculty of his fancy and incomparable force of his style were neither admired nor imitated." He made many observations on the character of the metaphors and comparisons, on the finished, determined and measured quality to be found in all the creations of Dante —in his Lucifer, for instance, so dissimilar from Milton's—but particularly in his mythology, which seemed to Macaulay to be antique and colossal in style, instinct with the spirit of Homer and Æschylus, rather than of Ovid and

Claudian.   He pronounced the Dantean Minos,
Charon and Pluto to be " absolutely appalling,"
and said that the use of classic names in the
" Inferno " " instils into the mind a vague and
tremendous idea of some mysterious revelation,
earlier than any written history, the dispersed
fragments of which have been preserved by
some means, despite imposture and superstition
of later religions."   He also began to throw
doubt on the traditional opinion that Dante's
poetry loses its force as it advances, growing
gradually less in passing from the " Inferno "
to the " Purgatorio," and from the " Purgatorio " to the " Paradiso."   Villemain considered that, owing to innate human incapacity
for representing felicity as truthfully as pain,
the " Paradiso " provided the poet with less
opportunity than the " Inferno," forcing him to
fall back upon a scholasticism, expressed indeed
with rare skill, but inevitably cold and tedious.
Coleridge preferred the " Inferno," because
Dante had been able to fill it far fuller with the
life of this world.   Fauriel, on the contrary,
whilst admitting the great beauties of the " Inferno," found incontestably greater beauties in
the other two poems.   Tommaseo thought the
beauties of the " Purgatorio " more pure and

more novel, and those of the " Paradiso " less
continuous but more intense and, after those to
be found in the Bible, " the most lofty that have
even been sung." Shelley held the " Purgatorio " to be a finer poem than the " Inferno,"
and in accordance with " critics of acute judgment," suggested that the vulgarly-accepted
valuation be reversed, rising from the " Inferno " to " Paradiso." Carlyle touched the
heart of the matter by declaring himself unable
to share the general preference of the day for
the " Inferno," and saying that in his opinion
such manifestations arose from " our generally
Byronic taste, which seems to be a passing
phase."

If the critical motive of the two Dantes and
the dual nature of the " Comedy," in which
Bouterweck saw a distinction between the
groundwork and the poetry of the poem, and
others with less exactitude, a conflict between
Dante the theologian and Dante the poet, does
not actually present the central problem of
Dantean criticism, it is at least a preliminary
problem demanding elucidation. Nobody
worked so continuously along this line as Francesco de Sanctis. His reflections on Dante
began in the Neapolitan lectures of 1842-43,

and were continued throughout the Turin lectures of 1854-55 and in a book on Dante which he never finished. Ten years later some of the material of this book was published as essays treating with the principal subjects of the " Inferno," and as a long chapter on the " Comedy " inserted in the " Storia della letteratura " of 1869-70.[1] It is therefore apparent that his investigations were never fully matured, being interrupted before being brought to a conclusion,—and this is to be remembered when reading the following remarks. Indeed, De Sanctis' solution of the problem was not very happy; the contrast between the two Dantes, variously considered by his predecessors, was conceived by him as lying between allegorism and poetry (or, as he was wont to say, between heaven and earth) whereas the true distinction exists (already perceived or dimly foreseen by Bouterweck), rather between groundwork and poetry. Consequently, De Sanctis describes Dante as " sublimely ignorant," unconscious of his own greatness. He was illogical in his methods, which, great poet though he was, often found themselves in involuntary and unconscious rebel-

[1] B. Croce, *Gli scritti di F. de Sanctis e la loro varia fortuna* (Bari, 1917), p. 30.

lion against his settled allegoristic intention, and allowed themselves to be overpowered by what De Sanctis calls " a beautiful untruth." The " Comedy " thus became what " mediæval ages realized as art, despite the author and despite his contemporaries." Such strife, however, may appear to our fancy as symbolic of the contrast between the reality of the poetry and the theories of Dante the critic, it is not to be found in Dante the poet. He habitually left allegory to externals. Sometimes, indeed, he interrupted his poetry in order to complete his purpose by using allegory, but having accomplished this, he rested upon his weapons (theories) and returned to his creations with the tranquil joy of the poet.

But in spite of his questionable theoretical explanations, De Sanctis was moved by the healthy impulse, common among romantic critics, to disengage Dante the poet from Dante the theologian, philosopher and practical man. He tried to judge him on his own merits. He also sought to draw criticism away from the allegory of the " Comedy," although he gave no exact definition of this mode of expression. His greatest merit is found when we compare him with the majority of romantic critics, who, in their haste to accomplish the above-mentioned liberation of poetry from non-poetry, threw away the religious and mystical element as unpoetical, preserving only the political and historical. For instance, Vischer, the German, a contemporary and colleague of De Sanctis, recalls in his " Æsthetic " Hegel's conception of the " Comedy " as a " religious epic " and points out that the form of the work is in contradiction to the essence of epic poetry, which demands a world of real humanity, concluding that only the " historical " portions may be considered poetical.[1] De Sanctis, on the contrary, whilst repudiating the allegorical religiosity, is not blind to the " concrete religiosity in the traditional and familiar figures," which exists in the poem and " is true poetry."[2] He analysed the cantos of Francesca, Farinata, Ugolino, and Pier della Vigna, as well as some portions of the " Purgatorio " and the " Paradiso," with a mastery unknown to his predecessors, making the reader feel their poetic beauty, thus surpassing for the first time both the

[1] *Æsthetik,* III., sec. II., p. 878, and for a conversation on the subject between De Sanctis and Vischer, see Croce, *Saggio sullo Hegel e altri scritti di storia della filosofia* (Bari, 1913), pp. 393-94.

[2] *Storia della letter. ital.,* ed. Croce, I, p. 167.

humanistic method of reducing the "beauties of Dante" to morsels (upon which argument Cesarotti had written a book), and the aphoristic and general method of the romantic critics, amongst whom Fauriel alone had attempted a detailed examination of the episodes in the "Comedy."

Owing to the great importance of such of his treatises as constitute real milestones in the history of Dantean studies, we must repeat that the general warning already given in the Introduction concerning the limits and defects of idealistic, æsthetic and romantic criticism, refers especially, *honoris causa,* to the Dantean criticism of De Sanctis. Whilst he was meditating the argument, he felt strongly the literary influences of romanticism and of the æsthetic Hegelian philosophies, from which he never entirely freed himself, although in later years he introduced into his critical method some rectifications in a "veristic" or romantic sense. He thus approached to a certain extent the state of mind stigmatised by Carlyle as "Byronic," in which the poetry of violent passion, that of the "Inferno," seems more poetic than that of the other two poems. According to him, this terrestrial life is presented in the "Inferno"

with absolute fidelity.   Sin is still alive there and
" the world " is still present to the damned.
Progress through the other two kingdoms, on
the other hand, is more and more abstract, and
is made from individual to species, from species
to genus.   Art becomes poor and flat, and the
figures of the " Purgatorio," neither agitated
nor passionate, have the beauty, but also the
monotony, of calm.   No longer do we have, as
in the " Inferno," great historic personalities,
powerful creatures of the imagination.   In De
Sanctis' opinion the chief poetical figures are
amongst the incontinent and violent, where the
world turns to tragedy and epic, Francesca and
Farinata.   He judges Francesca to be poetic
because she is a sinner and the poetry of
woman is in weakness, abandonment, sinfulness.
As we descend deeper into Hell, we find di-
minishing passion and increasing vice; we reach
negative beauty, ugliness, prose.   The only
artistic value here is the suggestion of the comic.
Consequently, the figures drawn rapidly by
Dante with only their salient characteristics,
seem to him to be indications calling for further
development.   They await a fuller life, to be
poured into them by Shakespeare and by all
modern literature; in themselves they are still

too undeveloped, too simple, too summary, too
abstract and immovable.[1]

De Sanctis held also to a realistic conception of artistic representation and thought the
" Inferno " suitable for representation and well
represented; he thought that the poet plucks
the heart of the reality amidst which he finds
himself. " For a Christian the life of the other
two worlds has no existence in reality, but is
pure imagination, composed of abstract duty
and reasoning." The " Paradiso " vaguely
glimpsed, may be art, but only as a
simple " lyric song " containing the uncertain
aspiration of the soul to the indefinable divine,"
not at all as " representation," owing to the
impossibility of a " description of that which is
beyond form." Somewhat materialistically, he
considered the other world as *materia signata,*
material more or less poetic in itself, possessed
of a certain sort of life, albeit a life surpassed
and immobilised, perfected by divine judgment,
devoid of chance and liberty (" the two chief
factors in real life and in art "). But, as has
been said already, he regarded it as graded

[1] Beside the close of the chapter on the *Commedia* in
Storia della letteratura and the essays on Francesca,
Farinata and Ugolino, see a passage in *Scrittivarî,* ed.
Croce, I., pp. 300-302 *n.*

downward æsthetically. Now and then he is
obliged to contradict himself; as when, for instance, he lifts his eyes from the " prose " of
Malebolge and beholds the tragic Ugolino and
the heroic Ulysses (whom he calls " the great
solitary man in Malebolge," thus striving to
hide his discomfiture!), or again when he feels
impelled to compare a method of representation
which occurs in certain of the circles (of money-
changers and false coiners) with an abstract
model (of the ludicrous), and to reprove Dante,
taking him to task as though the poet here were
forced and coldly comic, whereas the passages
have just that peculiar tone which they should
have for him who is in touch with the Dantean
spirit. In regard to the silent angel who trans-
ports the souls to the shore of Purgatory, there
is no need for his remarks that the figure " holds
a great place in the picture, but a small one in
the poetry," that he is " lacking in speech, lacking in personality, that he is the body of the
angel, not the angel himself." Such æsthetic
realism or " verism " verges on the arbitrary
idealisation of violent passion; by allowing the
subjectivity and individuality of poetry to vanish (that is to say, the lyrical characteristic
which is proper to it and determines its every

detail), it ends by conceiving Dantean poetry
as a work imperfectly executed, compared to
the supposed full representation of human reality attained by some (Shakespeare, Goethe,
Schiller). According to such criticism other
poets (Ariosto, Tasso, Alfieri) must be blamed
for not knowing how to improve on Dante in
this respect, or even for having gone backward
and created personages more or less abstract
and generic. We have, indeed, the wonder-
ing amazement of De Sanctis over the fact
that Silvio Polico, having before his eyes
Dante's Francesca as poetic source and living
model of " tenuous grace, charm and delicate
sentiment," should have depicted " a Francesca
so gross and coarse,"—as though Pellico could
possibly create a Francesca other than that conceived by his sentimental and patriotic, but ut-
terly unimaginative soul! Such defects of
method, of which many more instances could be
given, did not prevent De Sanctis, however,
from habitually feeling and estimating Dante's
poetry at its true value. It could be said of
him in this connection, far more correctly than
of Dante, that he deserves the praise of *felix
culpa,* of a beneficent incoherence and illogi-
cality.

The foregoing observations demonstrate in any case that although De Santis' work on Dante may serve as a powerful mental stimulus, it affords nothing conclusive, even in the narrowest sense of the term, in the way of solution for certain definite problems. It has posed or whetted the edges of more problems than it has solved or satisfied. In times immediately succeeding his, notwithstanding the large number of his Italian admirers (more from the point of view of art than of science), attention was distracted from these problems. A period of philologistic study (of history and literature), corresponding with the prevailing naturalism and philosophic positivism was beginning. This movement, with its incapacity for understanding spiritual creations, produced among other results a kind of obtuseness in critics. It restored allegorical and structural enquiries to the place of honour, especially such as are for the most part arbitrary and incapable of solution. As regards the early commentators, such questions suited the purposes of the men who read and expounded the poem (for it was expounded, sometimes even in the churches). In conformity with mediæval tradition, its allegorism was often interpreted rather piously than critically, as was the case with Schlosser, who, in full nineteenth century, confessed his need of piety and edification, and ingenuously declared that he had no desire to give learned information about Dante, but only to communicate " devout meditations on love and life, perfect wisdom and inner contemplation, and considerations on the divine essence and the intimate union of all things in the world."[1]   He deplores that " admiration of the poetry " should have cast " the old commentators " aside; he expresses a wish to return to them, above all to Landino and Vellutello, in whose writings he finds " grandeur and sublimity."   So also when the need for religious edification is replaced by that for civil or patriotic, such questions, sentimentally asked and answered in an imaginative manner, often have their practical value, as is seen in the Dantean literature of the national *Risorgimento,* in Rossetti, Gioberti, Tommaseo, Balbo, Rosmini, and many others.   In the prelude to Foscolo's illustrated edition of the " Comedy," Giuseppe Mazzini wrote: " We pygmies of to-day are unequal to understanding anything in Dante beyond the verse and the overwhelming imagination; some day, when we

[1] F. Ch. Schlosser, *Dante Studien* (Leipsic, 1855).

have become less unworthy of him, looking back
at the gigantic traces he imprinted on the paths
of social thought, we shall all go on a pilgrim-
age to Ravenna. We shall seek to draw from
the earth where lie his bones presages for our
fortune in days to come, and derive thence
strength to maintain ourselves on the heights
to which, ever since the fourteenth century, he
has directed the gaze of his compatriots."

Among the throng of arid men-of-letters,
grammarians, philologists and erudite persons,
acting as interpreters of Dante, it cannot be
denied that religious, political and humanita-
rian motives have been, and are, wanting. Save
in rare cases, their hermeneutic fancies lead to
nothing but moral sloth and mental incapacity,
and they recast and perpetuate traditions, not
those of pious souls and fervent patriots, but
those of frigid sixteenth and seventeenth century academicians, until they are best described
in the words of Bacon, as " fantastic, litigious
and ostentatious." I shall not linger to prepare
a sample or anthology of their favourite questions and discordant or uncertain answers (the
" serious problem " as they call it, of the
" steady foot "; another of the " three wild
beasts "; that of " five hundred, ten and five ";

and others), because the wish to laugh, and
make others laugh at them could be censured as
" base intent," in true Dantean style. It must
be confessed, too, that the spiritual ineptitude
and mental impotence of these " Dantean
scholars " is rather calculated to cause weariness
and repugnance and a sensation of distress such
as one feels at the sight of a deformity. Here
comes the " Danteist " who cannot unwind the
skein he himself has tangled, to whom none of
his colleagues, toiling at the same task, pays
attention when he tells them he has succeeded
in unravelling it and prides himself on his feat.
He is in turn thoughtful, heart-stricken, grieved,
bending under his load of responsibility; or he
is excited and fanatical, speaking and acting almost like a madman. Such is conspicuously the
case with one of them, by no means one of the
vulgar either. Pascoli never " conjectures " but
" sees "; does not discuss possibility or proba-
bility, but proclaims " definite and incontrovert-
ible truth." He wastes no time in persuasion,
through reasoning, but is " certain-sure." He
is consequently sometimes filled with " profound
gladness," bearing to Florence " in their earliest
lines, the thought of Dante and design of the
poem, which for six centuries have been un-

known and sought after." First to reveal " these deep mysteries," he is annoyed at the doubt and incredulity of others, and tells them such conduct " is an outrage, not to himself, but to the genius of our race," to Dante who deigns to speak through him. Quite recently, too, I received a book from a professor of statistics who, having become involved in the Dantean enigma, now persuades himself that he has found where lies not only the " secondary beauty " of Dante, but the " major part of his glories." He is convinced that he has " added greatly to the glory of Dante," and his joy is so boundless that he finishes with a hymn, whether to the praise of the discovery or of the discoverer it is difficult to say.[1]

These so-called " questions on Dante," for the most part quite unimportant and devoid of foundation and method, make up at least three-quarters of the immense mass of printed papers concerning the poet which have accumulated during the last fifty years. The remainder consists of philological enquiry into his life and times, and into the text of his works, its sources, and allusions. The allegories and true enigmas

[1] The title speaks for itself; R. Benini, *Dante tra gli splendori dei suoi enigmi risolti* (Rome, Sampaolesi, 1919).

in the poem have been treated, too, but historically, rather than imaginatively. It would be superfluous to point out the utility and legitimacy of such investigations, when undertaken by men of mark, from Witte to Moore, from Todeschini to Del Lungo, to mention but a few names. Yet great confusion exists among them when the poetry of the " Comedy " is considered. They do not make sufficient distinction between the historical interpretation we have named " allotrious," and the historico-æsthetic interpretation. Students of Dante still repeat and regard as incontestable that most mistaken notion that the premise, or " key," to the comprehension of Dante is a knowledge of his theology or philosophy, of his politics or biography. The truth is that while it is useful to know these and many other things historically, they must be regarded solely as a *function* of the poetry. In consequence, when learned students of one aspect of Dante are confronted with Dante the poet, they are helpless and, although provided as they believe themselves to be with many invaluable implements, they never seem able to lay hands on the one necessary to the understanding of the poetry. Lest we be suspected of talking idly, let anybody try to find

out what has been settled by the vast monograph on Dante by the German Kraus,[1] who
when he " reaches the point of comparison,"
when he should tell us what Dante's poetry
really is and describe what he calls " the æsthetic and rhetorical side of Dante," simply
refers us to the " special literature." The no
less vast and learned Italian monograph by
Zingarelli,[2] instead of an æsthetic study of
Dantean poetry, merely offers a classification
of the objects and emotions that Dante has represented, philological extracts from rhetorical
phrases and the like. Treatises on Dante in histories of literature, after having compiled the
biography and the external history of the
works, their sources, and the original traits and
general design of the " Comedy," say nothing
which has direct reference to the poetry, or
merely repeat general notions, when they do
not give a more or less insipid version of the
judgments of De Sanctis and other critics of the
romantic school.

It may be truly said that in order to understand Dante or any other creative spirit, over
and above familiar knowledge of this or that

[1] F. X. Kraus, *Dante, sein Leben, sein Werk, seine Ver-
hältnisse zur Kunst und zur Politik* (Berlin, 1897).

[2] *Dante* (Milan, Vallardi, 1903).

detail it is indispensable to possess a fundamental historic consciousness or conscience, which comes into being and grows with the formation and growth of our inner personality (a kind of ontogenesis coinciding with phylogenesis). In the case of Dante, it is necessary to create in ourselves a Dantean soul, and since he was a poet, to comprehend what poetry is in its eternal nature. If they do not fulfil these two conditions, the very finest intellects are unable to do more than sip poetry here and there, admire situations, words and images, dismiss some erroneous judgments, turn in the right direction, but never attack from the centre any of the problems raised by the subject. There are undoubtedly many beautiful pages, many acute observations to be found in the analytical essays of the last half-century on the " Comedy " and the other works of Dante. Particularly noteworthy are the " Dante Lectures," readings of single cantos with historical and æsthetic comments, held in Florence and other cities of Italy.[1] Some of them, unfortunately, lend themselves too easily to rhetorical effects and become diffuse over academic ques-

[1] Among the best is V. Spinazzola, *Il Canto XVII del Inferno* (Naples, 1903), on the figure of Geryon.

tions, minor erudition, paltry moral and political aims, quibbles and mutual admiration, and
in the æsthetic part, mince too fine. If we were
here writing a formal account of such studies,
mention would have to be made of exegeses
valuable for their æsthetic observations (such
as Torraca's commentary), as well as several
well-balanced introductions to the study of
Dante, such as that published some time ago by
the Englishman, Symonds, and the more recent
French one by Hauvette. There are the attempts at profound research such as that
concerning Dante's allegorism by Borinski, [1]
in a very heavy book, and concerning his
" subjectivism " by Gorra,[2] although this author
is not successful in keeping clear the distinction
between the various meanings of words, such as
" autobiographism," " lyricism " and " literary
class " when used of the lyric. Superior to these
works, the product of philology and the schools,
are the writings upon Dante of a man of letters and political journalist, the Polish refugee
Klaczko.[3] With acute penetration and nice

[1] K. Borinski, *Ueber poetische Vision und Imagination*
(Halle a/s 1897).

[2] E. Gorra, *Il soggettivismo di Dante* (Bologna, Zanichelli,
1899).

[3] J. Klaczko, *Causeries Florentines* (Paris, 1880).

sense of art, he takes up the old familiar comparison of Dante with Michelangelo and differentiates between the two artists, placing them in opposition one to the other. One of them, the sculptor, was the victim of an æsthetic tragedy, that of inadequacy of form to inspiration, of power of execution to imagination; the other was simply an artist who suffered a purely political tragedy, nourishing in his breast an ideal belonging to the past, not only discordant with contemporary life and the course of history, but rendered increasingly so according as it was opposed, attacked and corroded in every part by his own actions and his own intellectual and moral character. Reading these pages, wherein the artist speaks of the artist and the man of the man, we find ourselves in the company of Dante.

And finally, we are again in Dante's company with the latest great monograph upon the " Comedy," that of Vossler [1] although it embraces far more subjects than seem to be necessary. In the first three parts Vossler investigates the religious, philosophical, ethical, political and literary origins of Dantean thought and

[1] Karl Vossler, *Die göttliche Komödie, Entwicklungsgeschichte und Erklärung,* Heidelberg, 1907-10).

culture, going back to remote times, to oriental and Graeco-Roman antiquity and giving a general history of all these aspects of the human spirit throughout the long course of the ages, rather than a personal account of Dante. An immense amount of material is treated concisely and epigrammatically; sight is never lost of the ultimate object, the mind and soul of the author to be illustrated, the poet of the " Comedy." There is no exaggeration of Dante's worth as thinker, scientist, politician or religious man, and Vossler expressly recognises the scant originality of that which, rather than creating and transforming, Dante collected and comprised in his personality. He refuses to think of the " Comedy " as a " mixed work," a uniting of science with poetry; for as he well says, " the most powerful works of the mind of man are pure art, pure science, pure praxis." The last volume of the work is devoted entirely to the artistic problem of the " Comedy." Here the critic, whether consciously or not, does not follow out the consequences of his preceding volume, but begins a new work of criticism entirely afresh. He does not study Dante in his extra-poetic aspects, but examines the dialectic of Dante the artist and, indeed, gives the first

place to consideration of the problem of the
unity of the " Comedy." This problem it is
impossible to neglect, or to elude by making
mystical or intellectualistic assertions as to the
unity of the Dantean spirit. It presents itself
irresistibly to the notice of any poetically-minded
reader of the poem, and the history of Dantean
criticism shows that it has always been recognised and more or less successfully formulated
and solved. Vossler is fully conscious of it and
attacks it with great seriousness and energy,
recognising a duality and something like an
antinomy and strife between the ideal and the
real Dante; between the Dante who wishes to
change and correct himself, and the Dante who
does not change. Substantially this differs but
little from the distinction we ourselves have
drawn between Dante the author of a theological romance (the word " romance " would not
please Vossler, but the adjective " theological "
invests it with that seriousness and " realism "
he so rightly feels in Dantean creation), and
Dante the poet. There are even better things
in store; Vossler knows that the " fundamental
tone " of the style of the " Comedy " is " essentially lyrical," arising from the soul and feeling (*Gemüt*) of the " historical Dante Ali-

ghieri," but only to the extent that it is expressed
in the poem. But he also thinks that this vital
lyric principle, finding itself faced by the epico-
dramatic action of the " Comedy " (or, as we
should say, the theological romance, the voyage
through the three worlds), sometimes converts
it into true poetry and sometimes does not, and
that the æsthetic criticism of the poem should
consist of the examination of this strife and
change running through the three poems. It
will thus, according to Vossler's habitual practice, make exhaustive enquiry, poem by poem,
part by part, first into the bony structure, the
scenario, the contrivance, then into the external
action, proceeding in conclusion " to understand
and judge the propriety of these two factors,
starting from the propriety of the interior
action, the lyrical substratum of the poem."
In consequence of this view, Vossler finds that
the interpenetration of external and internal is
very marked in the " Inferno," less so in the
" Purgatorio," and non-existent in the " Paradiso," which he declares unhesitatingly to be a
" poetical contradiction," " a work fundament-
ally null," a " gigantic mistake." In conformity with this view, he is able to find poetical
justification for the penalties and punishments

and for interpolated passages, which are not in-
terpolations (as, for example, the lengthy political invective following the meeting with Sordello), and, more frequently, to find fault with
perfectly poetical parts, such as the figure of
Matelda amongst " the great variety of fresh
May-flowers," or the examination to which the
poet is subjected by the three apostles. Finally,
he ridicules the " Purgatorio " as a " cure-
house " or " sanatorium," and he calls the characters of the first canto of the " Paradiso "
" medical cases." It must be confessed that
some of Vossler's observations on other parts
of the poem are very acute, either when he
interprets its poetry or, as in the " Paradiso,"
when he shows how much is abstract and artificial, even superficial and pompous, in the
spectacles depicted. But his theory of the relation existing between structure and poetry is a
net which hinders him sorely and drags him towards the erroneous conclusions above mentioned, which logically followed would lead him
to portray Dante precisely in the way rejected
by Klaczko, as a poet struggling in an " æsthetic
tragedy," striving against sordid matter, now
victorious, now overcome. Such a conclusion is
entirely at variance with the physiognomy of

Dantean art, so purely outlined in its vigorous power. We must adopt, in order to escape these difficulties and errors, a hard and fast distinction between structure and poetry, always placing them in a strictly philosophic and ethical relation, and thus exhibiting the necessity of both, whilst not allowing to them any sort of relation of a purely poetical nature. This is the only way in which to enjoy fully the poetry of the " Comedy " to accept its structure, with a certain amount of indifference, perhaps, but without aversion and, above all, without derision.

The work of Vossler, excellent in nearly all its premises and rich in well-considered judgments,[1] should have shown the way to a better method of criticism of Dante. That this should not have been the case, that his fourth volume should have been little discussed and scarcely noticed, redounds little to the honour of Dantean studies, and affords clear proof of the sluggish mental energy with which they are generally prosecuted. This essay of mine has been written in the hope that it may lead to a better method. It has partly taken up the threads of

[1] The author informs me that he has prepared a new study on the " Paradiso " modifying his earlier judgment.

former criticisms and continued the web already woven, while elsewhere it has unwoven and introduced fresh threads, perhaps of more enduring nature. This contribution to the history of Dantean criticism—regarded from the point of view of interpretation and judgment of the poetry, is not to be confounded with the history of " allotrious " interpretation or with that of the " fortunes " of Dante—it is intended merely as an essay and a sign-post. It will perhaps be useful to have present to our minds in clearer detail what has up till now been definitely achieved or outlined or proposed in relation to the poetry of Dante, in order that we may link more closely new thoughts with old, and firmly establish, in this branch of study also, the chain of mental progress.

INDEX